Index

Important Notice

These tables cover the main rates of tax announced in the Chancellor's Budget speech on 21 March 2012 and included in the Finance Bill 2012. The rates apply for 2012/13 and for the corporation tax financial year 2012.

1

D1797153

How to use these tables for pence

These tables can be used for calculation in £, in pence, or in a combination of £ and pence.

Examples:

Page 6   20% of £28 = £5·60
            20% of 28p = 5·6p = 6p to nearest penny.

Page 19   What is the VAT content at 20% of an inclusive price of £50·83p?

$$£50·00 = \quad\quad £8·33$$
$$\underline{0·83} = 13·83p = \underline{0·14}$$
$$£50·83 = \quad\quad £8·47$$

General Editor
Mark McLaughlin CTA (Fellow) ATT TEP, Tax Consultant

Original Contributors
Personal tax
Sarah Laing CTA, Technical Author
Jennifer Adams FCIS TEP ATT, Technical Author

Pensions
Alec Ure and Tim Webb of Alec Ure & Associates

Corporate tax
Pete Miller CTA (Fellow), Partner, The Miller Partnership
Jennifer Adams FCIS TEP ATT, Technical Author

VAT
Andrew Needham BA CTA, VAT Specialists Limited

Customs duties
Jerry Wellens, for VAT Advisers Ltd

Stamp taxes
Shimon Shaw, Matthew Arnold & Baldwin LLP

Anti-avoidance
Shimon Shaw, Matthew Arnold & Baldwin LLP
Pete Miller CTA (Fellow), Partner, The Miller Partnership
Alec Ure and Tim Webb of Alec Ure & Associates

HMRC administration
Jennifer Adams FCIS TEP ATT, Technical Author

Bloomsbury Professional

Maxwelton House, 41–43 Boltro Road,
Haywards Heath, West Sussex, RH16 1BJ

© Bloomsbury Professional Ltd 2012.
Bloomsbury Professional, an imprint of Bloomsbury Publishing Plc

ISBN 978 184766 963 6

Typeset by Phoenix Photosetting, Chatham, Kent
Printed and bound in Great Britain by Fulmar

Gifts to Charities – net cost for individuals from 6 April 2012

By donations via Gift Aid and by deduction from pay under the Payroll Giving Schemes.

Net cost table (by Gross amount received by Charity)

Gross amount received by Charity £	Net cost to Donor, Top rate of income tax 20% £	40% £	Gross by amount received by Charity £	Net cost to Donor, Top rate of income tax 20% £	40% £
1	0·80	0·60	51	40·80	30·60
2	1·60	1·20	52	41·60	31·20
3	2·40	1·80	53	42·40	31·80
4	3·20	2·40	54	43·20	32·40
5	4·00	3·00	55	44·00	33·00
6	4·80	3·60	56	44·80	33·60
7	5·60	4·20	57	45·60	34·20
8	6·40	4·80	58	46·40	34·80
9	7·20	5·40	59	47·20	35·40
10	8·00	6·00	60	48·00	36·00
11	8·80	6·60	61	48·80	36·60
12	9·60	7·20	62	49·60	37·20
13	10·40	7·80	63	50·40	37·80
14	11·20	8·40	64	51·20	38·40
15	12·00	9·00	65	52·00	39·00
16	12·80	9·60	66	52·80	39·60
17	13·60	10·20	67	53·60	40·20
18	14·40	10·80	68	54·40	40·80
19	15·20	11·40	69	55·20	41·40
20	16·00	12·00	70	56·00	42·00
21	16·80	12·60	71	56·80	42·60
22	17·60	13·20	72	57·60	43·20
23	18·40	13·80	73	58·40	43·80
24	19·20	14·40	74	59·20	44·40
25	20·00	15·00	75	60·00	45·00
26	20·80	15·60	76	60·80	45·60
27	21·60	16·20	77	61·60	46·20
28	22·40	16·80	78	62·40	46·80
29	23·20	17·40	79	63·20	47·40
30	24·00	18·00	80	64·00	48·00
31	24·80	18·60	81	64·80	48·60
32	25·60	19·20	82	65·60	49·20
33	26·40	19·80	83	66·40	49·80
34	27·20	20·40	84	67·20	50·40
35	28·00	21·00	85	68·00	51·00
36	28·80	21·60	86	68·80	51·60
37	29·60	22·20	87	69·60	52·20
38	30·40	22·80	88	70·40	52·80
39	31·20	23·40	89	71·20	53·40
40	32·00	24·00	90	72·00	54·00
41	32·80	24·60	91	72·80	54·60
42	33·60	25·20	92	73·60	55·20
43	34·40	25·80	93	74·40	55·80
44	35·20	26·40	94	75·20	56·40
45	36·00	27·00	95	76·00	57·00
46	36·80	27·60	96	76·80	57·60
47	37·60	28·20	97	77·60	58·20
48	38·40	28·80	98	78·40	58·80
49	39·20	29·40	99	79·20	59·40
50	40·00	30·00	100	80·00	60·00

Gross amount table (by Net cost to Donor)

Net cost to Donor £	Gross amount received by Charity, if Donor's top rate of income tax 20% £	40% £	Net cost to Donor £	Gross amount received by Charity, if Donor's top rate of income tax 20% £	40% £
1	1·25	1·67	51	63·75	85·00
2	2·50	3·33	52	65·00	86·67
3	3·75	5·00	53	66·25	88·33
4	5·00	6·67	54	67·50	90·00
5	6·25	8·33	55	68·75	91·67
6	7·50	10·00	56	70·00	93·33
7	8·75	11·67	57	71·25	95·00
8	10·00	13·33	58	72·50	96·67
9	11·25	15·00	59	73·75	98·33
10	12·50	16·67	60	75·00	100·00
11	13·75	18·33	61	76·25	101·67
12	15·00	20·00	62	77·50	103·33
13	16·25	21·67	63	78·75	105·00
14	17·50	23·33	64	80·00	106·67
15	18·75	25·00	65	81·25	108·33
16	20·00	26·67	66	82·50	110·00
17	21·25	28·33	67	83·75	111·67
18	22·50	30·00	68	85·00	113·33
19	23·75	31·67	69	86·25	115·00
20	25·00	33·33	70	87·50	116·67
21	26·25	35·00	71	88·75	118·33
22	27·50	36·67	72	90·00	120·00
23	28·75	38·33	73	91·25	121·67
24	30·00	40·00	74	92·50	123·33
25	31·25	41·67	75	93·75	125·00
26	32·50	43·33	76	95·00	126·67
27	33·75	45·00	77	96·25	128·33
28	35·00	46·67	78	97·50	130·00
29	36·25	48·33	79	98·75	131·67
30	37·50	50·00	80	100·00	133·33
31	38·75	51·67	81	101·25	135·00
32	40·00	53·33	82	102·50	136·67
33	41·25	55·00	83	103·75	138·33
34	42·50	56·67	84	105·00	140·00
35	43·75	58·33	85	106·25	141·67
36	45·00	60·00	86	107·50	143·33
37	46·25	61·67	87	108·75	145·00
38	47·50	63·33	88	110·00	146·67
39	48·75	65·00	89	111·25	148·33
40	50·00	66·67	90	112·50	150·00
41	51·25	68·33	91	113·75	151·67
42	52·50	70·00	92	115·00	153·33
43	53·75	71·67	93	116·25	155·00
44	55·00	73·33	94	117·50	156·67
45	56·25	75·00	95	118·75	158·33
46	57·50	76·67	96	120·00	160·00
47	58·75	78·33	97	121·25	161·67
48	60·00	80·00	98	122·50	163·33
49	61·25	81·67	99	123·75	165·00
50	62·50	83·33	100	125·00	166·67

10% 2012/13: Income Tax (a)
Rate for capital gains qualifying for Entrepreneurs' Relief (b)

(a) Payable on the first £2,710 of savings income only and on dividend income within basic rate band.
(b) Applies from 23 June 2010.

£ or p	Tax £ or p	£ or p	Tax £ or p	£	Tax £	£	Tax £	£	Tax £	£	Tax £	£	Tax £	£	Tax £	£	Tax £	£	Tax £
1	0·10	51	5·10	101	10·10	151	15·10	201	20·10	251	25·10	301	30·10	351	35·10	401	40·10	451	45·10
2	0·20	52	5·20	102	10·20	152	15·20	202	20·20	252	25·20	302	30·20	352	35·20	402	40·20	452	45·20
3	0·30	53	5·30	103	10·30	153	15·30	203	20·30	253	25·30	303	30·30	353	35·30	403	40·30	453	45·30
4	0·40	54	5·40	104	10·40	154	15·40	204	20·40	254	25·40	304	30·40	354	35·40	404	40·40	454	45·40
5	0·50	55	5·50	105	10·50	155	15·50	205	20·50	255	25·50	305	30·50	355	35·50	405	40·50	455	45·50
6	0·60	56	5·60	106	10·60	156	15·60	206	20·60	256	25·60	306	30·60	356	35·60	406	40·60	456	45·60
7	0·70	57	5·70	107	10·70	157	15·70	207	20·70	257	25·70	307	30·70	357	35·70	407	40·70	457	45·70
8	0·80	58	5·80	108	10·80	158	15·80	208	20·80	258	25·80	308	30·80	358	35·80	408	40·80	458	45·80
9	0·90	59	5·90	109	10·90	159	15·90	209	20·90	259	25·90	309	30·90	359	35·90	409	40·90	459	45·90
10	1·00	60	6·00	110	11·00	160	16·00	210	21·00	260	26·00	310	31·00	360	36·00	410	41·00	460	46·00
11	1·10	61	6·10	111	11·10	161	16·10	211	21·10	261	26·10	311	31·10	361	36·10	411	41·10	461	46·10
12	1·20	62	6·20	112	11·20	162	16·20	212	21·20	262	26·20	312	31·20	362	36·20	412	41·20	462	46·20
13	1·30	63	6·30	113	11·30	163	16·30	213	21·30	263	26·30	313	31·30	363	36·30	413	41·30	463	46·30
14	1·40	64	6·40	114	11·40	164	16·40	214	21·40	264	26·40	314	31·40	364	36·40	414	41·40	464	46·40
15	1·50	65	6·50	115	11·50	165	16·50	215	21·50	265	26·50	315	31·50	365	36·50	415	41·50	465	46·50
16	1·60	66	6·60	116	11·60	166	16·60	216	21·60	266	26·60	316	31·60	366	36·60	416	41·60	466	46·60
17	1·70	67	6·70	117	11·70	167	16·70	217	21·70	267	26·70	317	31·70	367	36·70	417	41·70	467	46·70
18	1·80	68	6·80	118	11·80	168	16·80	218	21·80	268	26·80	318	31·80	368	36·80	418	41·80	468	46·80
19	1·90	69	6·90	119	11·90	169	16·90	219	21·90	269	26·90	319	31·90	369	36·90	419	41·90	469	46·90
20	2·00	70	7·00	120	12·00	170	17·00	220	22·00	270	27·00	320	32·00	370	37·00	420	42·00	470	47·00
21	2·10	71	7·10	121	12·10	171	17·10	221	22·10	271	27·10	321	32·10	371	37·10	421	42·10	471	47·10
22	2·20	72	7·20	122	12·20	172	17·20	222	22·20	272	27·20	322	32·20	372	37·20	422	42·20	472	47·20
23	2·30	73	7·30	123	12·30	173	17·30	223	22·30	273	27·30	323	32·30	373	37·30	423	42·30	473	47·30
24	2·40	74	7·40	124	12·40	174	17·40	224	22·40	274	27·40	324	32·40	374	37·40	424	42·40	474	47·40
25	2·50	75	7·50	125	12·50	175	17·50	225	22·50	275	27·50	325	32·50	375	37·50	425	42·50	475	47·50
26	2·60	76	7·60	126	12·60	176	17·60	226	22·60	276	27·60	326	32·60	376	37·60	426	42·60	476	47·60
27	2·70	77	7·70	127	12·70	177	17·70	227	22·70	277	27·70	327	32·70	377	37·70	427	42·70	477	47·70
28	2·80	78	7·80	128	12·80	178	17·80	228	22·80	278	27·80	328	32·80	378	37·80	428	42·80	478	47·80
29	2·90	79	7·90	129	12·90	179	17·90	229	22·90	279	27·90	329	32·90	379	37·90	429	42·90	479	47·90
30	3·00	80	8·00	130	13·00	180	18·00	230	23·00	280	28·00	330	33·00	380	38·00	430	43·00	480	48·00
31	3·10	81	8·10	131	13·10	181	18·10	231	23·10	281	28·10	331	33·10	381	38·10	431	43·10	481	48·10
32	3·20	82	8·20	132	13·20	182	18·20	232	23·20	282	28·20	332	33·20	382	38·20	432	43·20	482	48·20
33	3·30	83	8·30	133	13·30	183	18·30	233	23·30	283	28·30	333	33·30	383	38·30	433	43·30	483	48·30
34	3·40	84	8·40	134	13·40	184	18·40	234	23·40	284	28·40	334	33·40	384	38·40	434	43·40	484	48·40
35	3·50	85	8·50	135	13·50	185	18·50	235	23·50	285	28·50	335	33·50	385	38·50	435	43·50	485	48·50
36	3·60	86	8·60	136	13·60	186	18·60	236	23·60	286	28·60	336	33·60	386	38·60	436	43·60	486	48·60
37	3·70	87	8·70	137	13·70	187	18·70	237	23·70	287	28·70	337	33·70	387	38·70	437	43·70	487	48·70
38	3·80	88	8·80	138	13·80	188	18·80	238	23·80	288	28·80	338	33·80	388	38·80	438	43·80	488	48·80
39	3·90	89	8·90	139	13·90	189	18·90	239	23·90	289	28·90	339	33·90	389	38·90	439	43·90	489	48·90
40	4·00	90	9·00	140	14·00	190	19·00	240	24·00	290	29·00	340	34·00	390	39·00	440	44·00	490	49·00
41	4·10	91	9·10	141	14·10	191	19·10	241	24·10	291	29·10	341	34·10	391	39·10	441	44·10	491	49·10
42	4·20	92	9·20	142	14·20	192	19·20	242	24·20	292	29·20	342	34·20	392	39·20	442	44·20	492	49·20
43	4·30	93	9·30	143	14·30	193	19·30	243	24·30	293	29·30	343	34·30	393	39·30	443	44·30	493	49·30
44	4·40	94	9·40	144	14·40	194	19·40	244	24·40	294	29·40	344	34·40	394	39·40	444	44·40	494	49·40
45	4·50	95	9·50	145	14·50	195	19·50	245	24·50	295	29·50	345	34·50	395	39·50	445	44·50	495	49·50
46	4·60	96	9·60	146	14·60	196	19·60	246	24·60	296	29·60	346	34·60	396	39·60	446	44·60	496	49·60
47	4·70	97	9·70	147	14·70	197	19·70	247	24·70	297	29·70	347	34·70	397	39·70	447	44·70	497	49·70
48	4·80	98	9·80	148	14·80	198	19·80	248	24·80	298	29·80	348	34·80	398	39·80	448	44·80	498	49·80
49	4·90	99	9·90	149	14·90	199	19·90	249	24·90	299	29·90	349	34·90	399	39·90	449	44·90	499	49·90
50	5·00	100	10·00	150	15·00	200	20·00	250	25·00	300	30·00	350	35·00	400	40·00	450	45·00	500	50·00
On Tax		£1,000 £100		£1,500 £150		£2,000 £200		£2,500 £250		£3,000 £300		£3,500 £350		£4,000 £400		£4,500 £450		£5,000 £500	

Capital Gains Tax Rate 2012/13 18%

£ or p	Tax £ or p	£ or p	Tax £ or p	£	Tax £	£	Tax £	£	Tax £	£	Tax £	£	Tax £	£	Tax £	£	Tax £	£	Tax £
1	0·18	51	9·18	101	18·18	151	27·18	201	36·18	251	45·18	301	54·18	351	63·18	401	72·18	451	81·18
2	0·36	52	9·36	102	18·36	152	27·36	202	36·36	252	45·36	302	54·36	352	63·36	402	72·36	452	81·36
3	0·54	53	9·54	103	18·54	153	27·54	203	36·54	253	45·54	303	54·54	353	63·54	403	72·54	453	81·54
4	0·72	54	9·72	104	18·72	154	27·72	204	36·72	254	45·72	304	54·72	354	63·72	404	72·72	454	81·72
5	0·90	55	9·90	105	18·90	155	27·90	205	36·90	255	45·90	305	54·90	355	63·90	405	72·90	455	81·90
6	1·08	56	10·08	106	19·08	156	28·08	206	37·08	256	46·08	306	55·08	356	64·08	406	73·08	456	82·08
7	1·26	57	10·26	107	19·26	157	28·26	207	37·26	257	46·26	307	55·26	357	64·26	407	73·26	457	82·26
8	1·44	58	10·44	108	19·44	158	28·44	208	37·44	258	46·44	308	55·44	358	64·44	408	73·44	458	82·44
9	1·62	59	10·62	109	19·62	159	28·62	209	37·62	259	46·62	309	55·62	359	64·62	409	73·62	459	82·62
10	1·80	60	10·80	110	19·80	160	28·80	210	37·80	260	46·80	310	55·80	360	64·80	410	73·80	460	82·80
11	1·98	61	10·98	111	19·98	161	28·98	211	37·98	261	46·98	311	55·98	361	64·98	411	73·98	461	82·98
12	2·16	62	11·16	112	20·16	162	29·16	212	38·16	262	47·16	312	56·16	362	65·16	412	74·16	462	83·16
13	2·34	63	11·34	113	20·34	163	29·34	213	38·34	263	47·34	313	56·34	363	65·34	413	74·34	463	83·34
14	2·52	64	11·52	114	20·52	164	29·52	214	38·52	264	47·52	314	56·52	364	65·52	414	74·52	464	83·52
15	2·70	65	11·70	115	20·70	165	29·70	215	38·70	265	47·70	315	56·70	365	65·70	415	74·70	465	83·70
16	2·88	66	11·88	116	20·88	166	29·88	216	38·88	266	47·88	316	56·88	366	65·88	416	74·88	466	83·88
17	3·06	67	12·06	117	21·06	167	30·06	217	39·06	267	48·06	317	57·06	367	66·06	417	75·06	467	84·06
18	3·24	68	12·24	118	21·24	168	30·24	218	39·24	268	48·24	318	57·24	368	66·24	418	75·24	468	84·24
19	3·42	69	12·42	119	21·42	169	30·42	219	39·42	269	48·42	319	57·42	369	66·42	419	75·42	469	84·42
20	3·60	70	12·60	120	21·60	170	30·60	220	39·60	270	48·60	320	57·60	370	66·60	420	75·60	470	84·60
21	3·78	71	12·78	121	21·78	171	30·78	221	39·78	271	48·78	321	57·78	371	66·78	421	75·78	471	84·78
22	3·96	72	12·96	122	21·96	172	30·96	222	39·96	272	48·96	322	57·96	372	66·96	422	75·96	472	84·96
23	4·14	73	13·14	123	22·14	173	31·14	223	40·14	273	49·14	323	58·14	373	67·14	423	76·14	473	85·14
24	4·32	74	13·32	124	22·32	174	31·32	224	40·32	274	49·32	324	58·32	374	67·32	424	76·32	474	85·32
25	4·50	75	13·50	125	22·50	175	31·50	225	40·50	275	49·50	325	58·50	375	67·50	425	76·50	475	85·50
26	4·68	76	13·68	126	22·68	176	31·68	226	40·68	276	49·68	326	58·68	376	67·68	426	76·68	476	85·68
27	4·86	77	13·86	127	22·86	177	31·86	227	40·86	277	49·86	327	58·86	377	67·86	427	76·86	477	85·86
28	5·04	78	14·04	128	23·04	178	32·04	228	41·04	278	50·04	328	59·04	378	68·04	428	77·04	478	86·04
29	5·22	79	14·22	129	23·22	179	32·22	229	41·22	279	50·22	329	59·22	379	68·22	429	77·22	479	86·22
30	5·40	80	14·40	130	23·40	180	32·40	230	41·40	280	50·40	330	59·40	380	68·40	430	77·40	480	86·40
31	5·58	81	14·58	131	23·58	181	32·58	231	41·58	281	50·58	331	59·58	381	68·58	431	77·58	481	86·58
32	5·76	82	14·76	132	23·76	182	32·76	232	41·76	282	50·76	332	59·76	382	68·76	432	77·76	482	86·76
33	5·94	83	14·94	133	23·94	183	32·94	233	41·94	283	50·94	333	59·94	383	68·94	433	77·94	483	86·94
34	6·12	84	15·12	134	24·12	184	33·12	234	42·12	284	51·12	334	60·12	384	69·12	434	78·12	484	87·12
35	6·30	85	15·30	135	24·30	185	33·30	235	42·30	285	51·30	335	60·30	385	69·30	435	78·30	485	87·30
36	6·48	86	15·48	136	24·48	186	33·48	236	42·48	286	51·48	336	60·48	386	69·48	436	78·48	486	87·48
37	6·66	87	15·66	137	24·66	187	33·66	237	42·66	287	51·66	337	60·66	387	69·66	437	78·66	487	87·66
38	6·84	88	15·84	138	24·84	188	33·84	238	42·84	288	51·84	338	60·84	388	69·84	438	78·84	488	87·84
39	7·02	89	16·02	139	25·02	189	34·02	239	43·02	289	52·02	339	61·02	389	70·02	439	79·02	489	88·02
40	7·20	90	16·20	140	25·20	190	34·20	240	43·20	290	52·20	340	61·20	390	70·20	440	79·20	490	88·20
41	7·38	91	16·38	141	25·38	191	34·38	241	43·38	291	52·38	341	61·38	391	70·38	441	79·38	491	88·38
42	7·56	92	16·56	142	25·56	192	34·56	242	43·56	292	52·56	342	61·56	392	70·56	442	79·56	492	88·56
43	7·74	93	16·74	143	25·74	193	34·74	243	43·74	293	52·74	343	61·74	393	70·74	443	79·74	493	88·74
44	7·92	94	16·92	144	25·92	194	34·92	244	43·92	294	52·92	344	61·92	394	70·92	444	79·92	494	88·92
45	8·10	95	17·10	145	26·10	195	35·10	245	44·10	295	53·10	345	62·10	395	71·10	445	80·10	495	89·10
46	8·28	96	17·28	146	26·28	196	35·28	246	44·28	296	53·28	346	62·28	396	71·28	446	80·28	496	89·28
47	8·46	97	17·46	147	26·46	197	35·46	247	44·46	297	53·46	347	62·46	397	71·46	447	80·46	497	89·46
48	8·64	98	17·64	148	26·64	198	35·64	248	44·64	298	53·64	348	62·64	398	71·64	448	80·64	498	89·64
49	8·82	99	17·82	149	26·82	199	35·82	249	44·82	299	53·82	349	62·82	399	71·82	449	80·82	499	89·82
50	9·00	100	18·00	150	27·00	200	36·00	250	45·00	300	54·00	350	63·00	400	72·00	450	81·00	500	90·00

On Tax	£1,000 £180	£1,500 £270	£2,000 £360	£2,500 £450	£3,000 £540	£3,500 £630	£4,000 £720	£4,500 £810	£5,000 £900

20%   Basic Rate 2012/13 Income Tax (a)
Corporation Tax: Small Profits Rate F.Y. 2012 (b)

(a) Payable on savings and non-savings income (if 10% band exceeded) up to £34,370.

(b) Rate of corporation tax payable on taxable profits not exceeding £300,000.

£ or p	Tax £ or p	£ or p	Tax £ or p	£	Tax £	£	Tax £	£	Tax £	£	Tax £	£	Tax £	£	Tax £	£	Tax £	£	Tax £
1	0·20	51	10·20	101	20·20	151	30·20	201	40·20	251	50·20	301	60·20	351	70·20	401	80·20	451	90·20
2	0·40	52	10·40	102	20·40	152	30·40	202	40·40	252	50·40	302	60·40	352	70·40	402	80·40	452	90·40
3	0·60	53	10·60	103	20·60	153	30·60	203	40·60	253	50·60	303	60·60	353	70·60	403	80·60	453	90·60
4	0·80	54	10·80	104	20·80	154	30·80	204	40·80	254	50·80	304	60·80	354	70·80	404	80·80	454	90·80
5	1·00	55	11·00	105	21·00	155	31·00	205	41·00	255	51·00	305	61·00	355	71·00	405	81·00	455	91·00
6	1·20	56	11·20	106	21·20	156	31·20	206	41·20	256	51·20	306	61·20	356	71·20	406	81·20	456	91·20
7	1·40	57	11·40	107	21·40	157	31·40	207	41·40	257	51·40	307	61·40	357	71·40	407	81·40	457	91·40
8	1·60	58	11·60	108	21·60	158	31·60	208	41·60	258	51·60	308	61·60	358	71·60	408	81·60	458	91·60
9	1·80	59	11·80	109	21·80	159	31·80	209	41·80	259	51·80	309	61·80	359	71·80	409	81·80	459	91·80
10	2·00	60	12·00	110	22·00	160	32·00	210	42·00	260	52·00	310	62·00	360	72·00	410	82·00	460	92·00
11	2·20	61	12·20	111	22·20	161	32·20	211	42·20	261	52·20	311	62·20	361	72·20	411	82·20	461	92·20
12	2·40	62	12·40	112	22·40	162	32·40	212	42·40	262	52·40	312	62·40	362	72·40	412	82·40	462	92·40
13	2·60	63	12·60	113	22·60	163	32·60	213	42·60	263	52·60	313	62·60	363	72·60	413	82·60	463	92·60
14	2·80	64	12·80	114	22·80	164	32·80	214	42·80	264	52·80	314	62·80	364	72·80	414	82·80	464	92·80
15	3·00	65	13·00	115	23·00	165	33·00	215	43·00	265	53·00	315	63·00	365	73·00	415	83·00	465	93·00
16	3·20	66	13·20	116	23·20	166	33·20	216	43·20	266	53·20	316	63·20	366	73·20	416	83·20	466	93·20
17	3·40	67	13·40	117	23·40	167	33·40	217	43·40	267	53·40	317	63·40	367	73·40	417	83·40	467	93·40
18	3·60	68	13·60	118	23·60	168	33·60	218	43·60	268	53·60	318	63·60	368	73·60	418	83·60	468	93·60
19	3·80	69	13·80	119	23·80	169	33·80	219	43·80	269	53·80	319	63·80	369	73·80	419	83·80	469	93·80
20	4·00	70	14·00	120	24·00	170	34·00	220	44·00	270	54·00	320	64·00	370	74·00	420	84·00	470	94·00
21	4·20	71	14·20	121	24·20	171	34·20	221	44·20	271	54·20	321	64·20	371	74·20	421	84·20	471	94·20
22	4·40	72	14·40	122	24·40	172	34·40	222	44·40	272	54·40	322	64·40	372	74·40	422	84·40	472	94·40
23	4·60	73	14·60	123	24·60	173	34·60	223	44·60	273	54·60	323	64·60	373	74·60	423	84·60	473	94·60
24	4·80	74	14·80	124	24·80	174	34·80	224	44·80	274	54·80	324	64·80	374	74·80	424	84·80	474	94·80
25	5·00	75	15·00	125	25·00	175	35·00	225	45·00	275	55·00	325	65·00	375	75·00	425	85·00	475	95·00
26	5·20	76	15·20	126	25·20	176	35·20	226	45·20	276	55·20	326	65·20	376	75·20	426	85·20	476	95·20
27	5·40	77	15·40	127	25·40	177	35·40	227	45·40	277	55·40	327	65·40	377	75·40	427	85·40	477	95·40
28	5·60	78	15·60	128	25·60	178	35·60	228	45·60	278	55·60	328	65·60	378	75·60	428	85·60	478	95·60
29	5·80	79	15·80	129	25·80	179	35·80	229	45·80	279	55·80	329	65·80	379	75·80	429	85·80	479	95·80
30	6·00	80	16·00	130	26·00	180	36·00	230	46·00	280	56·00	330	66·00	380	76·00	430	86·00	480	96·00
31	6·20	81	16·20	131	26·20	181	36·20	231	46·20	281	56·20	331	66·20	381	76·20	431	86·20	481	96·20
32	6·40	82	16·40	132	26·40	182	36·40	232	46·40	282	56·40	332	66·40	382	76·40	432	86·40	482	96·40
33	6·60	83	16·60	133	26·60	183	36·60	233	46·60	283	56·60	333	66·60	383	76·60	433	86·60	483	96·60
34	6·80	84	16·80	134	26·80	184	36·80	234	46·80	284	56·80	334	66·80	384	76·80	434	86·80	484	96·80
35	7·00	85	17·00	135	27·00	185	37·00	235	47·00	285	57·00	335	67·00	385	77·00	435	87·00	485	97·00
36	7·20	86	17·20	136	27·20	186	37·20	236	47·20	286	57·20	336	67·20	386	77·20	436	87·20	486	97·20
37	7·40	87	17·40	137	27·40	187	37·40	237	47·40	287	57·40	337	67·40	387	77·40	437	87·40	487	97·40
38	7·60	88	17·60	138	27·60	188	37·60	238	47·60	288	57·60	338	67·60	388	77·60	438	87·60	488	97·60
39	7·80	89	17·80	139	27·80	189	37·80	239	47·80	289	57·80	339	67·80	389	77·80	439	87·80	489	97·80
40	8·00	90	18·00	140	28·00	190	38·00	240	48·00	290	58·00	340	68·00	390	78·00	440	88·00	490	98·00
41	8·20	91	18·20	141	28·20	191	38·20	241	48·20	291	58·20	341	68·20	391	78·20	441	88·20	491	98·20
42	8·40	92	18·40	142	28·40	192	38·40	242	48·40	292	58·40	342	68·40	392	78·40	442	88·40	492	98·40
43	8·60	93	18·60	143	28·60	193	38·60	243	48·60	293	58·60	343	68·60	393	78·60	443	88·60	493	98·60
44	8·80	94	18·80	144	28·80	194	38·80	244	48·80	294	58·80	344	68·80	394	78·80	444	88·80	494	98·80
45	9·00	95	19·00	145	29·00	195	39·00	245	49·00	295	59·00	345	69·00	395	79·00	445	89·00	495	99·00
46	9·20	96	19·20	146	29·20	196	39·20	246	49·20	296	59·20	346	69·20	396	79·20	446	89·20	496	99·20
47	9·40	97	19·40	147	29·40	197	39·40	247	49·40	297	59·40	347	69·40	397	79·40	447	89·40	497	99·40
48	9·60	98	19·60	148	29·60	198	39·60	248	49·60	298	59·60	348	69·60	398	79·60	448	89·60	498	99·60
49	9·80	99	19·80	149	29·80	199	39·80	249	49·80	299	59·80	349	69·80	399	79·80	449	89·80	499	99·80
50	10·00	100	20·00	150	30·00	200	40·00	250	50·00	300	60·00	350	70·00	400	80·00	450	90·00	500	100·00

On Tax	£1,000 £200	£1,500 £300	£2,000 £400	£2,500 £500	£3,000 £600	£3,500 £700	£4,000 £800	£4,500 £900	£5,000 £1,000

Rate of corporation tax payable on taxable profits of £1,500,000 and over for financial year 2012

Corporation Tax: Full Rate F.Y. 2012   24%

£ or p	Tax £ or p	£ or p	Tax £ or p	£	Tax £	£	Tax £	£	Tax £	£	Tax £	£	Tax £	£	Tax £	£	Tax £	£	Tax £
1	0.24	51	12.24	101	24.24	151	36.24	201	48.24	251	60.24	301	72.24	351	84.24	401	96.24	451	108.24
2	0.48	52	12.48	102	24.48	152	36.48	202	48.48	252	60.48	302	72.48	352	84.48	402	96.48	452	108.48
3	0.72	53	12.72	103	24.72	153	36.72	203	48.72	253	60.72	303	72.72	353	84.72	403	96.72	453	108.72
4	0.96	54	12.96	104	24.96	154	36.96	204	48.96	254	60.96	304	72.96	354	84.96	404	96.96	454	108.96
5	1.20	55	13.20	105	25.20	155	37.20	205	49.20	255	61.20	305	73.20	355	85.20	405	97.20	455	109.20
6	1.44	56	13.44	106	25.44	156	37.44	206	49.44	256	61.44	306	73.44	356	85.44	406	97.44	456	109.44
7	1.68	57	13.68	107	25.68	157	37.68	207	49.68	257	61.68	307	73.68	357	85.68	407	97.68	457	109.68
8	1.92	58	13.92	108	25.92	158	37.92	208	49.92	258	61.92	308	73.92	358	85.92	408	97.92	458	109.92
9	2.16	59	14.16	109	26.16	159	38.16	209	50.16	259	62.16	309	74.16	359	86.16	409	98.16	459	110.16
10	2.40	60	14.40	110	26.40	160	38.40	210	50.40	260	62.40	310	74.40	360	86.40	410	98.40	460	110.40
11	2.64	61	14.64	111	26.64	161	38.64	211	50.64	261	62.64	311	74.64	361	86.64	411	98.64	461	110.64
12	2.88	62	14.88	112	26.88	162	38.88	212	50.88	262	62.88	312	74.88	362	86.88	412	98.88	462	110.88
13	3.12	63	15.12	113	27.12	163	39.12	213	51.12	263	63.12	313	75.12	363	87.12	413	99.12	463	111.12
14	3.36	64	15.36	114	27.36	164	39.36	214	51.36	264	63.36	314	75.36	364	87.36	414	99.36	464	111.36
15	3.60	65	15.60	115	27.60	165	39.60	215	51.60	265	63.60	315	75.60	365	87.60	415	99.60	465	111.60
16	3.84	66	15.84	116	27.84	166	39.84	216	51.84	266	63.84	316	75.84	366	87.84	416	99.84	466	111.84
17	4.08	67	16.08	117	28.08	167	40.08	217	52.08	267	64.08	317	76.08	367	88.08	417	100.08	467	112.08
18	4.32	68	16.32	118	28.32	168	40.32	218	52.32	268	64.32	318	76.32	368	88.32	418	100.32	468	112.32
19	4.56	69	16.56	119	28.56	169	40.56	219	52.56	269	64.56	319	76.56	369	88.56	419	100.56	469	112.56
20	4.80	70	16.80	120	28.80	170	40.80	220	52.80	270	64.80	320	76.80	370	88.80	420	100.80	470	112.80
21	5.04	71	17.04	121	29.04	171	41.04	221	53.04	271	65.04	321	77.04	371	89.04	421	101.04	471	113.04
22	5.28	72	17.28	122	29.28	172	41.28	222	53.28	272	65.28	322	77.28	372	89.28	422	101.28	472	113.28
23	5.52	73	17.52	123	29.52	173	41.52	223	53.52	273	65.52	323	77.52	373	89.52	423	101.52	473	113.52
24	5.76	74	17.76	124	29.76	174	41.76	224	53.76	274	65.76	324	77.76	374	89.76	424	101.76	474	113.76
25	6.00	75	18.00	125	30.00	175	42.00	225	54.00	275	66.00	325	78.00	375	90.00	425	102.00	475	114.00
26	6.24	76	18.24	126	30.24	176	42.24	226	54.24	276	66.24	326	78.24	376	90.24	426	102.24	476	114.24
27	6.48	77	18.48	127	30.48	177	42.48	227	54.48	277	66.48	327	78.48	377	90.48	427	102.48	477	114.48
28	6.72	78	18.72	128	30.72	178	42.72	228	54.72	278	66.72	328	78.72	378	90.72	428	102.72	478	114.72
29	6.96	79	18.96	129	30.96	179	42.96	229	54.96	279	66.96	329	78.96	379	90.96	429	102.96	479	114.96
30	7.20	80	19.20	130	31.20	180	43.20	230	55.20	280	67.20	330	79.20	380	91.20	430	103.20	480	115.20
31	7.44	81	19.44	131	31.44	181	43.44	231	55.44	281	67.44	331	79.44	381	91.44	431	103.44	481	115.44
32	7.68	82	19.68	132	31.68	182	43.68	232	55.68	282	67.68	332	79.68	382	91.68	432	103.68	482	115.68
33	7.92	83	19.92	133	31.92	183	43.92	233	55.92	283	67.92	333	79.92	383	91.92	433	103.92	483	115.92
34	8.16	84	20.16	134	32.16	184	44.16	234	56.16	284	68.16	334	80.16	384	92.16	434	104.16	484	116.16
35	8.40	85	20.40	135	32.40	185	44.40	235	56.40	285	68.40	335	80.40	385	92.40	435	104.40	485	116.40
36	8.64	86	20.64	136	32.64	186	44.64	236	56.64	286	68.64	336	80.64	386	92.64	436	104.64	486	116.64
37	8.88	87	20.88	137	32.88	187	44.88	237	56.88	287	68.88	337	80.88	387	92.88	437	104.88	487	116.88
38	9.12	88	21.12	138	33.12	188	45.12	238	57.12	288	69.12	338	81.12	388	93.12	438	105.12	488	117.12
39	9.36	89	21.36	139	33.36	189	45.36	239	57.36	289	69.36	339	81.36	389	93.36	439	105.36	489	117.36
40	9.60	90	21.60	140	33.60	190	45.60	240	57.60	290	69.60	340	81.60	390	93.60	440	105.60	490	117.60
41	9.84	91	21.84	141	33.84	191	45.84	241	57.84	291	69.84	341	81.84	391	93.84	441	105.84	491	117.84
42	10.08	92	22.08	142	34.08	192	46.08	242	58.08	292	70.08	342	82.08	392	94.08	442	106.08	492	118.08
43	10.32	93	22.32	143	34.32	193	46.32	243	58.32	293	70.32	343	82.32	393	94.32	443	106.32	493	118.32
44	10.56	94	22.56	144	34.56	194	46.56	244	58.56	294	70.56	344	82.56	394	94.56	444	106.56	494	118.56
45	10.80	95	22.80	145	34.80	195	46.80	245	58.80	295	70.80	345	82.80	395	94.80	445	106.80	495	118.80
46	11.04	96	23.04	146	35.04	196	47.04	246	59.04	296	71.04	346	83.04	396	95.04	446	107.04	496	119.04
47	11.28	97	23.28	147	35.28	197	47.28	247	59.28	297	71.28	347	83.28	397	95.28	447	107.28	497	119.28
48	11.52	98	23.52	148	35.52	198	47.52	248	59.52	298	71.52	348	83.52	398	95.52	448	107.52	498	119.52
49	11.76	99	23.76	149	35.76	199	47.76	249	59.76	299	71.76	349	83.76	399	95.76	449	107.76	499	119.76
50	12.00	100	24.00	150	36.00	200	48.00	250	60.00	300	72.00	350	84.00	400	96.00	450	108.00	500	120.00
On Tax	**£1,000** £240		**£1,500** £360		**£2,000** £480		**£2,500** £600		**£3,000** £720		**£3,500** £840		**£4,000** £960		**£4,500** £1,080		**£5,000** £1,200		

25% Corporation Tax: Small Profits Marginal Rate F.Y. 2012

Rate of corporation tax payable on taxable profits of £1,500,000 and over for financial year 2012.

£ or p	Tax £ or p	£ or p	Tax £ or p	£	Tax £	£	Tax £	£	Tax £	£	Tax £	£	Tax £	£	Tax £	£	Tax £	£	Tax £
1	0.25	51	12.75	101	25.25	151	37.75	201	50.25	251	62.75	301	75.25	351	87.75	401	100.25	451	112.75
2	0.50	52	13.00	102	25.50	152	38.00	202	50.50	252	63.00	302	75.50	352	88.00	402	100.50	452	113.00
3	0.75	53	13.25	103	25.75	153	38.25	203	50.75	253	63.25	303	75.75	353	88.25	403	100.75	453	113.25
4	1.00	54	13.50	104	26.00	154	38.50	204	51.00	254	63.50	304	76.00	354	88.50	404	101.00	454	113.50
5	1.25	55	13.75	105	26.25	155	38.75	205	51.25	255	63.75	305	76.25	355	88.75	405	101.25	455	113.75
6	1.50	56	14.00	106	26.50	156	39.00	206	51.50	256	64.00	306	76.50	356	89.00	406	101.50	456	114.00
7	1.75	57	14.25	107	26.75	157	39.25	207	51.75	257	64.25	307	76.75	357	89.25	407	101.75	457	114.25
8	2.00	58	14.50	108	27.00	158	39.50	208	52.00	258	64.50	308	77.00	358	89.50	408	102.00	458	114.50
9	2.25	59	14.75	109	27.25	159	39.75	209	52.25	259	64.75	309	77.25	359	89.75	409	102.25	459	114.75
10	2.50	60	15.00	110	27.50	160	40.00	210	52.50	260	65.00	310	77.50	360	90.00	410	102.50	460	115.00
11	2.75	61	15.25	111	27.75	161	40.25	211	52.75	261	65.25	311	77.75	361	90.25	411	102.75	461	115.25
12	3.00	62	15.50	112	28.00	162	40.50	212	53.00	262	65.50	312	78.00	362	90.50	412	103.00	462	115.50
13	3.25	63	15.75	113	28.25	163	40.75	213	53.25	263	65.75	313	78.25	363	90.75	413	103.25	463	115.75
14	3.50	64	16.00	114	28.50	164	41.00	214	53.50	264	66.00	314	78.50	364	91.00	414	103.50	464	116.00
15	3.75	65	16.25	115	28.75	165	41.25	215	53.75	265	66.25	315	78.75	365	91.25	415	103.75	465	116.25
16	4.00	66	16.50	116	29.00	166	41.50	216	54.00	266	66.50	316	79.00	366	91.50	416	104.00	466	116.50
17	4.25	67	16.75	117	29.25	167	41.75	217	54.25	267	66.75	317	79.25	367	91.75	417	104.25	467	116.75
18	4.50	68	17.00	118	29.50	168	42.00	218	54.50	268	67.00	318	79.50	368	92.00	418	104.50	468	117.00
19	4.75	69	17.25	119	29.75	169	42.25	219	54.75	269	67.25	319	79.75	369	92.25	419	104.75	469	117.25
20	5.00	70	17.50	120	30.00	170	42.50	220	55.00	270	67.50	320	80.00	370	92.50	420	105.00	470	117.50
21	5.25	71	17.75	121	30.25	171	42.75	221	55.25	271	67.75	321	80.25	371	92.75	421	105.25	471	117.75
22	5.50	72	18.00	122	30.50	172	43.00	222	55.50	272	68.00	322	80.50	372	93.00	422	105.50	472	118.00
23	5.75	73	18.25	123	30.75	173	43.25	223	55.75	273	68.25	323	80.75	373	93.25	423	105.75	473	118.25
24	6.00	74	18.50	124	31.00	174	43.50	224	56.00	274	68.50	324	81.00	374	93.50	424	106.00	474	118.50
25	6.25	75	18.75	125	31.25	175	43.75	225	56.25	275	68.75	325	81.25	375	93.75	425	106.25	475	118.75
26	6.50	76	19.00	126	31.50	176	44.00	226	56.50	276	69.00	326	81.50	376	94.00	426	106.50	476	119.00
27	6.75	77	19.25	127	31.75	177	44.25	227	56.75	277	69.25	327	81.75	377	94.25	427	106.75	477	119.25
28	7.00	78	19.50	128	32.00	178	44.50	228	57.00	278	69.50	328	82.00	378	94.50	428	107.00	478	119.50
29	7.25	79	19.75	129	32.25	179	44.75	229	57.25	279	69.75	329	82.25	379	94.75	429	107.25	479	119.75
30	7.50	80	20.00	130	32.50	180	45.00	230	57.50	280	70.00	330	82.50	380	95.00	430	107.50	480	120.00
31	7.75	81	20.25	131	32.75	181	45.25	231	57.75	281	70.25	331	82.75	381	95.25	431	107.75	481	120.25
32	8.00	82	20.50	132	33.00	182	45.50	232	58.00	282	70.50	332	83.00	382	95.50	432	108.00	482	120.50
33	8.25	83	20.75	133	33.25	183	45.75	233	58.25	283	70.75	333	83.25	383	95.75	433	108.25	483	120.75
34	8.50	84	21.00	134	33.50	184	46.00	234	58.50	284	71.00	334	83.50	384	96.00	434	108.50	484	121.00
35	8.75	85	21.25	135	33.75	185	46.25	235	58.75	285	71.25	335	83.75	385	96.25	435	108.75	485	121.25
36	9.00	86	21.50	136	34.00	186	46.50	236	59.00	286	71.50	336	84.00	386	96.50	436	109.00	486	121.50
37	9.25	87	21.75	137	34.25	187	46.75	237	59.25	287	71.75	337	84.25	387	96.75	437	109.25	487	121.75
38	9.50	88	22.00	138	34.50	188	47.00	238	59.50	288	72.00	338	84.50	388	97.00	438	109.50	488	122.00
39	9.75	89	22.25	139	34.75	189	47.25	239	59.75	289	72.25	339	84.75	389	97.25	439	109.75	489	122.25
40	10.00	90	22.50	140	35.00	190	47.50	240	60.00	290	72.50	340	85.00	390	97.50	440	110.00	490	122.50
41	10.25	91	22.75	141	35.25	191	47.75	241	60.25	291	72.75	341	85.25	391	97.75	441	110.25	491	122.75
42	10.50	92	23.00	142	35.50	192	48.00	242	60.50	292	73.00	342	85.50	392	98.00	442	110.50	492	123.00
43	10.75	93	23.25	143	35.75	193	48.25	243	60.75	293	73.25	343	85.75	393	98.25	443	110.75	493	123.25
44	11.00	94	23.50	144	36.00	194	48.50	244	61.00	294	73.50	344	86.00	394	98.50	444	111.00	494	123.50
45	11.25	95	23.75	145	36.25	195	48.75	245	61.25	295	73.75	345	86.25	395	98.75	445	111.25	495	123.75
46	11.50	96	24.00	146	36.50	196	49.00	246	61.50	296	74.00	346	86.50	396	99.00	446	111.50	496	124.00
47	11.75	97	24.25	147	36.75	197	49.25	247	61.75	297	74.25	347	86.75	397	99.25	447	111.75	497	124.25
48	12.00	98	24.50	148	37.00	198	49.50	248	62.00	298	74.50	348	87.00	398	99.50	448	112.00	498	124.50
49	12.25	99	24.75	149	37.25	199	49.75	249	62.25	299	74.75	349	87.25	399	99.75	449	112.25	499	124.75
50	12.50	100	25.00	150	37.50	200	50.00	250	62.50	300	75.00	350	87.50	400	100.00	450	112.50	500	125.00

On	£1,000	£1,500	£2,000	£2,500	£3,000	£3,500	£4,000	£4,500	£5,000
Tax	£250	£375	£500	£625	£750	£875	£1,000	£1,125	£1,250

Applies to gains (or part of gains) above the upper limit of the income tax basic rate band. Also applies to trustees and personal representatives.

Higher Rate Capital Gains Tax Rate 28%

£ or p	Tax £ or p	£ or p	Tax £ or p	£	Tax £	£	Tax £	£	Tax £	£	Tax £	£	Tax £	£	Tax £	£	Tax £	£	Tax £
1	0·28	51	14·28	101	28·28	151	42·28	201	56·28	251	70·28	301	84·28	351	98·28	401	112·28	451	126·28
2	0·56	52	14·56	102	28·56	152	42·56	202	56·56	252	70·56	302	84·56	352	98·56	402	112·56	452	126·56
3	0·84	53	14·84	103	28·84	153	42·84	203	56·84	253	70·84	303	84·84	353	98·84	403	112·84	453	126·84
4	1·12	54	15·12	104	29·12	154	43·12	204	57·12	254	71·12	304	85·12	354	99·12	404	113·12	454	127·12
5	1·40	55	15·40	105	29·40	155	43·40	205	57·40	255	71·40	305	85·40	355	99·40	405	113·40	455	127·40
6	1·68	56	15·68	106	29·68	156	43·68	206	57·68	256	71·68	306	85·68	356	99·68	406	113·68	456	127·68
7	1·96	57	15·96	107	29·96	157	43·96	207	57·96	257	71·96	307	85·96	357	99·96	407	113·96	457	127·96
8	2·24	58	16·24	108	30·24	158	44·24	208	58·24	258	72·24	308	86·24	358	100·24	408	114·24	458	128·24
9	2·52	59	16·52	109	30·52	159	44·52	209	58·52	259	72·52	309	86·52	359	100·52	409	114·52	459	128·52
10	2·80	60	16·80	110	30·80	160	44·80	210	58·80	260	72·80	310	86·80	360	100·80	410	114·80	460	128·80
11	3·08	61	17·08	111	31·08	161	45·08	211	59·08	261	73·08	311	87·08	361	101·08	411	115·08	461	129·08
12	3·36	62	17·36	112	31·36	162	45·36	212	59·36	262	73·36	312	87·36	362	101·36	412	115·36	462	129·36
13	3·64	63	17·64	113	31·64	163	45·64	213	59·64	263	73·64	313	87·64	363	101·64	413	115·64	463	129·64
14	3·92	64	17·92	114	31·92	164	45·92	214	59·92	264	73·92	314	87·92	364	101·92	414	115·92	464	129·92
15	4·20	65	18·20	115	32·20	165	46·20	215	60·20	265	74·20	315	88·20	365	102·20	415	116·20	465	130·20
16	4·48	66	18·48	116	32·48	166	46·48	216	60·48	266	74·48	316	88·48	366	102·48	416	116·48	466	130·48
17	4·76	67	18·76	117	32·76	167	46·76	217	60·76	267	74·76	317	88·76	367	102·76	417	116·76	467	130·76
18	5·04	68	19·04	118	33·04	168	47·04	218	61·04	268	75·04	318	89·04	368	103·04	418	117·04	468	131·04
19	5·32	69	19·32	119	33·32	169	47·32	219	61·32	269	75·32	319	89·32	369	103·32	419	117·32	469	131·32
20	5·60	70	19·60	120	33·60	170	47·60	220	61·60	270	75·60	320	89·60	370	103·60	420	117·60	470	131·60
21	5·88	71	19·88	121	33·88	171	47·88	221	61·88	271	75·88	321	89·88	371	103·88	421	117·88	471	131·88
22	6·16	72	20·16	122	34·16	172	48·16	222	62·16	272	76·16	322	90·16	372	104·16	422	118·16	472	132·16
23	6·44	73	20·44	123	34·44	173	48·44	223	62·44	273	76·44	323	90·44	373	104·44	423	118·44	473	132·44
24	6·72	74	20·72	124	34·72	174	48·72	224	62·72	274	76·72	324	90·72	374	104·72	424	118·72	474	132·72
25	7·00	75	21·00	125	35·00	175	49·00	225	63·00	275	77·00	325	91·00	375	105·00	425	119·00	475	133·00
26	7·28	76	21·28	126	35·28	176	49·28	226	63·28	276	77·28	326	91·28	376	105·28	426	119·28	476	133·28
27	7·56	77	21·56	127	35·56	177	49·56	227	63·56	277	77·56	327	91·56	377	105·56	427	119·56	477	133·56
28	7·84	78	21·84	128	35·84	178	49·84	228	63·84	278	77·84	328	91·84	378	105·84	428	119·84	478	133·84
29	8·12	79	22·12	129	36·12	179	50·12	229	64·12	279	78·12	329	92·12	379	106·12	429	120·12	479	134·12
30	8·40	80	22·40	130	36·40	180	50·40	230	64·40	280	78·40	330	92·40	380	106·40	430	120·40	480	134·40
31	8·68	81	22·68	131	36·68	181	50·68	231	64·68	281	78·68	331	92·68	381	106·68	431	120·68	481	134·68
32	8·96	82	22·96	132	36·96	182	50·96	232	64·96	282	78·96	332	92·96	382	106·96	432	120·96	482	134·96
33	9·24	83	23·24	133	37·24	183	51·24	233	65·24	283	79·24	333	93·24	383	107·24	433	121·24	483	135·24
34	9·52	84	23·52	134	37·52	184	51·52	234	65·52	284	79·52	334	93·52	384	107·52	434	121·52	484	135·52
35	9·80	85	23·80	135	37·80	185	51·80	235	65·80	285	79·80	335	93·80	385	107·80	435	121·80	485	135·80
36	10·08	86	24·08	136	38·08	186	52·08	236	66·08	286	80·08	336	94·08	386	108·08	436	122·08	486	136·08
37	10·36	87	24·36	137	38·36	187	52·36	237	66·36	287	80·36	337	94·36	387	108·36	437	122·36	487	136·36
38	10·64	88	24·64	138	38·64	188	52·64	238	66·64	288	80·64	338	94·64	388	108·64	438	122·64	488	136·64
39	10·92	89	24·92	139	38·92	189	52·92	239	66·92	289	80·92	339	94·92	389	108·92	439	122·92	489	136·92
40	11·20	90	25·20	140	39·20	190	53·20	240	67·20	290	81·20	340	95·20	390	109·20	440	123·20	490	137·20
41	11·48	91	25·48	141	39·48	191	53·48	241	67·48	291	81·48	341	95·48	391	109·48	441	123·48	491	137·48
42	11·76	92	25·76	142	39·76	192	53·76	242	67·76	292	81·76	342	95·76	392	109·76	442	123·76	492	137·76
43	12·04	93	26·04	143	40·04	193	54·04	243	68·04	293	82·04	343	96·04	393	110·04	443	124·04	493	138·04
44	12·32	94	26·32	144	40·32	194	54·32	244	68·32	294	82·32	344	96·32	394	110·32	444	124·32	494	138·32
45	12·60	95	26·60	145	40·60	195	54·60	245	68·60	295	82·60	345	96·60	395	110·60	445	124·60	495	138·60
46	12·88	96	26·88	146	40·88	196	54·88	246	68·88	296	82·88	346	96·88	396	110·88	446	124·88	496	138·88
47	13·16	97	27·16	147	41·16	197	55·16	247	69·16	297	83·16	347	97·16	397	111·16	447	125·16	497	139·16
48	13·44	98	27·44	148	41·44	198	55·44	248	69·44	298	83·44	348	97·44	398	111·44	448	125·44	498	139·44
49	13·72	99	27·72	149	41·72	199	55·72	249	69·72	299	83·72	349	97·72	399	111·72	449	125·72	499	139·72
50	14·00	100	28·00	150	42·00	200	56·00	250	70·00	300	84·00	350	98·00	400	112·00	450	126·00	500	140·00

On Tax	£1,000 £280	£1,500 £420	£2,000 £560	£2,500 £700	£3,000 £840	£3,500 £980	£4,000 £1,120	£4,500 £1,260	£5,000 £1,400

32·5%   2012/13: Income Tax on Dividend Income

Payable by higher rate taxpayers on taxable income between £34,371 and £150,000.

£ or p	Tax £ or p	£ or p	Tax £ or p	£	Tax £	£	Tax £	£	Tax £	£	Tax £	£	Tax £	£	Tax £	£	Tax £	£	Tax £
1	0·33	51	16·58	101	32·83	151	49·08	201	65·33	251	81·58	301	97·83	351	114·08	401	130·33	451	146·58
2	0·65	52	16·90	102	33·15	152	49·40	202	65·65	252	81·90	302	98·15	352	114·40	402	130·65	452	146·90
3	0·98	53	17·23	103	33·48	153	49·73	203	65·98	253	82·23	303	98·48	353	114·73	403	130·98	453	147·23
4	1·30	54	17·55	104	33·80	154	50·05	204	66·30	254	82·55	304	98·80	354	115·05	404	131·30	454	147·55
5	1·63	55	17·88	105	34·13	155	50·38	205	66·63	255	82·88	305	99·13	355	115·38	405	131·63	455	147·88
6	1·95	56	18·20	106	34·45	156	50·70	206	66·95	256	83·20	306	99·45	356	115·70	406	131·95	456	148·20
7	2·28	57	18·53	107	34·78	157	51·03	207	67·28	257	83·53	307	99·78	357	116·03	407	132·28	457	148·53
8	2·60	58	18·85	108	35·10	158	51·35	208	67·60	258	83·85	308	100·10	358	116·35	408	132·60	458	148·85
9	2·93	59	19·18	109	35·43	159	51·68	209	67·93	259	84·18	309	100·43	359	116·68	409	132·93	459	149·18
10	3·25	60	19·50	110	35·75	160	52·00	210	68·25	260	84·50	310	100·75	360	117·00	410	133·25	460	149·50
11	3·58	61	19·83	111	36·08	161	52·33	211	68·58	261	84·83	311	101·08	361	117·33	411	133·58	461	149·83
12	3·90	62	20·15	112	36·40	162	52·65	212	68·90	262	85·15	312	101·40	362	117·65	412	133·90	462	150·15
13	4·23	63	20·48	113	36·73	163	52·98	213	69·23	263	85·48	313	101·73	363	117·98	413	134·23	463	150·48
14	4·55	64	20·80	114	37·05	164	53·30	214	69·55	264	85·80	314	102·05	364	118·30	414	134·55	464	150·80
15	4·88	65	21·13	115	37·38	165	53·63	215	69·88	265	86·13	315	102·38	365	118·63	415	134·88	465	151·13
16	5·20	66	21·45	116	37·70	166	53·95	216	70·20	266	86·45	316	102·70	366	118·95	416	135·20	466	151·45
17	5·53	67	21·78	117	38·03	167	54·28	217	70·53	267	86·78	317	103·03	367	119·28	417	135·53	467	151·78
18	5·85	68	22·10	118	38·35	168	54·60	218	70·85	268	87·10	318	103·35	368	119·60	418	135·85	468	152·10
19	6·18	69	22·43	119	38·68	169	54·93	219	71·18	269	87·43	319	103·68	369	119·93	419	136·18	469	152·43
20	6·50	70	22·75	120	39·00	170	55·25	220	71·50	270	87·75	320	104·00	370	120·25	420	136·50	470	152·75
21	6·83	71	23·08	121	39·33	171	55·58	221	71·83	271	88·08	321	104·33	371	120·58	421	136·83	471	153·08
22	7·15	72	23·40	122	39·65	172	55·90	222	72·15	272	88·40	322	104·65	372	120·90	422	137·15	472	153·40
23	7·48	73	23·73	123	39·98	173	56·23	223	72·48	273	88·73	323	104·98	373	121·23	423	137·48	473	153·73
24	7·80	74	24·05	124	40·30	174	56·55	224	72·80	274	89·05	324	105·30	374	121·55	424	137·80	474	154·05
25	8·13	75	24·38	125	40·63	175	56·88	225	73·13	275	89·38	325	105·63	375	121·88	425	138·13	475	154·38
26	8·45	76	24·70	126	40·95	176	57·20	226	73·45	276	89·70	326	105·95	376	122·20	426	138·45	476	154·70
27	8·78	77	25·03	127	41·28	177	57·53	227	73·78	277	90·03	327	106·28	377	122·53	427	138·78	477	155·03
28	9·10	78	25·35	128	41·60	178	57·85	228	74·10	278	90·35	328	106·60	378	122·85	428	139·10	478	155·35
29	9·43	79	25·68	129	41·93	179	58·18	229	74·43	279	90·68	329	106·93	379	123·18	429	139·43	479	155·68
30	9·75	80	26·00	130	42·25	180	58·50	230	74·75	280	91·00	330	107·25	380	123·50	430	139·75	480	156·00
31	10·08	81	26·33	131	42·58	181	58·83	231	75·08	281	91·33	331	107·58	381	123·83	431	140·08	481	156·33
32	10·40	82	26·65	132	42·90	182	59·15	232	75·40	282	91·65	332	107·90	382	124·15	432	140·40	482	156·65
33	10·73	83	26·98	133	43·23	183	59·48	233	75·73	283	91·98	333	108·23	383	124·48	433	140·73	483	156·98
34	11·05	84	27·30	134	43·55	184	59·80	234	76·05	284	92·30	334	108·55	384	124·80	434	141·05	484	157·30
35	11·38	85	27·63	135	43·88	185	60·13	235	76·38	285	92·63	335	108·88	385	125·13	435	141·38	485	157·63
36	11·70	86	27·95	136	44·20	186	60·45	236	76·70	286	92·95	336	109·20	386	125·45	436	141·70	486	157·95
37	12·03	87	28·28	137	44·53	187	60·78	237	77·03	287	93·28	337	109·53	387	125·78	437	142·03	487	158·28
38	12·35	88	28·60	138	44·85	188	61·10	238	77·35	288	93·60	338	109·85	388	126·10	438	142·35	488	158·60
39	12·68	89	28·93	139	45·18	189	61·43	239	77·68	289	93·93	339	110·18	389	126·43	439	142·68	489	158·93
40	13·00	90	29·25	140	45·50	190	61·75	240	78·00	290	94·25	340	110·50	390	126·75	440	143·00	490	159·25
41	13·33	91	29·58	141	45·83	191	62·08	241	78·33	291	94·58	341	110·83	391	127·08	441	143·33	491	159·58
42	13·65	92	29·90	142	46·15	192	62·40	242	78·65	292	94·90	342	111·15	392	127·40	442	143·65	492	159·90
43	13·98	93	30·23	143	46·48	193	62·73	243	78·98	293	95·23	343	111·48	393	127·73	443	143·98	493	160·23
44	14·30	94	30·55	144	46·80	194	63·05	244	79·30	294	95·55	344	111·80	394	128·05	444	144·30	494	160·55
45	14·63	95	30·88	145	47·13	195	63·38	245	79·63	295	95·88	345	112·13	395	128·38	445	144·63	495	160·88
46	14·95	96	31·20	146	47·45	196	63·70	246	79·95	296	96·20	346	112·45	396	128·70	446	144·95	496	161·20
47	15·28	97	31·53	147	47·78	197	64·03	247	80·28	297	96·53	347	112·78	397	129·03	447	145·28	497	161·53
48	15·60	98	31·85	148	48·10	198	64·35	248	80·60	298	96·85	348	113·10	398	129·35	448	145·60	498	161·85
49	15·93	99	32·18	149	48·43	199	64·68	249	80·93	299	97·18	349	113·43	399	129·68	449	145·93	499	162·18
50	16·25	100	32·50	150	48·75	200	65·00	250	81·25	300	97·50	350	113·75	400	130·00	450	146·25	500	162·50
On Tax		£1,000 £325		£1,500 £488		£2,000 £650		£2,500 £813		£3,000 £975		£3,500 £1,138		£4,000 £1,300		£4,500 £1,463		£5,000 £1,625	

Payable by higher rate taxpayers on taxable income between £34,371 and £150,000.

2012/13: Income Tax on Dividend Income 32·5%

£	Tax £	£	Tax £	£	Tax £	£	Tax £	£	Tax £	£	Tax £	£	Tax £	£	Tax £	£	Tax £	£	Tax £
501	162·83	551	179·08	601	195·33	651	211·58	701	227·83	751	244·08	801	260·33	851	276·58	901	292·83	951	309·08
502	163·15	552	179·40	602	195·65	652	211·90	702	228·15	752	244·40	802	260·65	852	276·90	902	293·15	952	309·40
503	163·48	553	179·73	603	195·98	653	212·23	703	228·48	753	244·73	803	260·98	853	277·23	903	293·48	953	309·73
504	163·80	554	180·05	604	196·30	654	212·55	704	228·80	754	245·05	804	261·30	854	277·55	904	293·80	954	310·05
505	164·13	555	180·38	605	196·63	655	212·88	705	229·13	755	245·38	805	261·63	855	277·88	905	294·13	955	310·38
506	164·45	556	180·70	606	196·95	656	213·20	706	229·45	756	245·70	806	261·95	856	278·20	906	294·45	956	310·70
507	164·78	557	181·03	607	197·28	657	213·53	707	229·78	757	246·03	807	262·28	857	278·53	907	294·78	957	311·03
508	165·10	558	181·35	608	197·60	658	213·85	708	230·10	758	246·35	808	262·60	858	278·85	908	295·10	958	311·35
509	165·43	559	181·68	609	197·93	659	214·18	709	230·43	759	246·68	809	262·93	859	279·18	909	295·43	959	311·68
510	165·75	560	182·00	610	198·25	660	214·50	710	230·75	760	247·00	810	263·25	860	279·50	910	295·75	960	312·00
511	166·08	561	182·33	611	198·58	661	214·83	711	231·08	761	247·33	811	263·58	861	279·83	911	296·08	961	312·33
512	166·40	562	182·65	612	198·90	662	215·15	712	231·40	762	247·65	812	263·90	862	280·15	912	296·40	962	312·65
513	166·73	563	182·98	613	199·23	663	215·48	713	231·73	763	247·98	813	264·23	863	280·48	913	296·73	963	312·98
514	167·05	564	183·30	614	199·55	664	215·80	714	232·05	764	248·30	814	264·55	864	280·80	914	297·05	964	313·30
515	167·38	565	183·63	615	199·88	665	216·13	715	232·38	765	248·63	815	264·88	865	281·13	915	297·38	965	313·63
516	167·70	566	183·95	616	200·20	666	216·45	716	232·70	766	248·95	816	265·20	866	281·45	916	297·70	966	313·95
517	168·03	567	184·28	617	200·53	667	216·78	717	233·03	767	249·28	817	265·53	867	281·78	917	298·03	967	314·28
518	168·35	568	184·60	618	200·85	668	217·10	718	233·35	768	249·60	818	265·85	868	282·10	918	298·35	968	314·60
519	168·68	569	184·93	619	201·18	669	217·43	719	233·68	769	249·93	819	266·18	869	282·43	919	298·68	969	314·93
520	169·00	570	185·25	620	201·50	670	217·75	720	234·00	770	250·25	820	266·50	870	282·75	920	299·00	970	315·25
521	169·33	571	185·58	621	201·83	671	218·08	721	234·33	771	250·58	821	266·83	871	283·08	921	299·33	971	315·58
522	169·65	572	185·90	622	202·15	672	218·40	722	234·65	772	250·90	822	267·15	872	283·40	922	299·65	972	315·90
523	169·98	573	186·23	623	202·48	673	218·73	723	234·98	773	251·23	823	267·48	873	283·73	923	299·98	973	316·23
524	170·30	574	186·55	624	202·80	674	219·05	724	235·30	774	251·55	824	267·80	874	284·05	924	300·30	974	316·55
525	170·63	575	186·88	625	203·13	675	219·38	725	235·63	775	251·88	825	268·13	875	284·38	925	300·63	975	316·88
526	170·95	576	187·20	626	203·45	676	219·70	726	235·95	776	252·20	826	268·45	876	284·70	926	300·95	976	317·20
527	171·28	577	187·53	627	203·78	677	220·03	727	236·28	777	252·53	827	268·78	877	285·03	927	301·28	977	317·53
528	171·60	578	187·85	628	204·10	678	220·35	728	236·60	778	252·85	828	269·10	878	285·35	928	301·60	978	317·85
529	171·93	579	188·18	629	204·43	679	220·68	729	236·93	779	253·18	829	269·43	879	285·68	929	301·93	979	318·18
530	172·25	580	188·50	630	204·75	680	221·00	730	237·25	780	253·50	830	269·75	880	286·00	930	302·25	980	318·50
531	172·58	581	188·83	631	205·08	681	221·33	731	237·58	781	253·83	831	270·08	881	286·33	931	302·58	981	318·83
532	172·90	582	189·15	632	205·40	682	221·65	732	237·90	782	254·15	832	270·40	882	286·65	932	302·90	982	319·15
533	173·23	583	189·48	633	205·73	683	221·98	733	238·23	783	254·48	833	270·73	883	286·98	933	303·23	983	319·48
534	173·55	584	189·80	634	206·05	684	222·30	734	238·55	784	254·80	834	271·05	884	287·30	934	303·55	984	319·80
535	173·88	585	190·13	635	206·38	685	222·63	735	238·88	785	255·13	835	271·38	885	287·63	935	303·88	985	320·13
536	174·20	586	190·45	636	206·70	686	222·95	736	239·20	786	255·45	836	271·70	886	287·95	936	304·20	986	320·45
537	174·53	587	190·78	637	207·03	687	223·28	737	239·53	787	255·78	837	272·03	887	288·28	937	304·53	987	320·78
538	174·85	588	191·10	638	207·35	688	223·60	738	239·85	788	256·10	838	272·35	888	288·60	938	304·85	988	321·10
539	175·18	589	191·43	639	207·68	689	223·93	739	240·18	789	256·43	839	272·68	889	288·93	939	305·18	989	321·43
540	175·50	590	191·75	640	208·00	690	224·25	740	240·50	790	256·75	840	273·00	890	289·25	940	305·50	990	321·75
541	175·83	591	192·08	641	208·33	691	224·58	741	240·83	791	257·08	841	273·33	891	289·58	941	305·83	991	322·08
542	176·15	592	192·40	642	208·65	692	224·90	742	241·15	792	257·40	842	273·65	892	289·90	942	306·15	992	322·40
543	176·48	593	192·73	643	208·98	693	225·23	743	241·48	793	257·73	843	273·98	893	290·23	943	306·48	993	322·73
544	176·80	594	193·05	644	209·30	694	225·55	744	241·80	794	258·05	844	274·30	894	290·55	944	306·80	994	323·05
545	177·13	595	193·38	645	209·63	695	225·88	745	242·13	795	258·38	845	274·63	895	290·88	945	307·13	995	323·38
546	177·45	596	193·70	646	209·95	696	226·20	746	242·45	796	258·70	846	274·95	896	291·20	946	307·45	996	323·70
547	177·78	597	194·03	647	210·28	697	226·53	747	242·78	797	259·03	847	275·28	897	291·53	947	307·78	997	324·03
548	178·10	598	194·35	648	210·60	698	226·85	748	243·10	798	259·35	848	275·60	898	291·85	948	308·10	998	324·35
549	178·43	599	194·68	649	210·93	699	227·18	749	243·43	799	259·68	849	275·93	899	292·18	949	308·43	999	324·68
550	178·75	600	195·00	650	211·25	700	227·50	750	243·75	800	260·00	850	276·25	900	292·50	950	308·75	1000	325·00

On Tax	£5,500 £1,788	£6,000 £1,950	£6,500 £2,113	£7,000 £2,275	£7,500 £2,438	£8,000 £2,600	£8,500 £2,763	£9,000 £2,925	£9,500 £3,088

40% 2012/13: Income Tax (a) Inheritance Tax (b)

(a) Payable on taxable income between £34,371 and £150,000.
(b) Payable on chargeable transfers over £325,000.

£ or p	Tax £ or p	£ or p	Tax £ or p	£	Tax £	£	Tax £	£	Tax £	£	Tax £	£	Tax £	£	Tax £	£	Tax £	£	Tax £
1	0·40	51	20·40	101	40·40	151	60·40	201	80·40	251	100·40	301	120·40	351	140·40	401	160·40	451	180·40
2	0·80	52	20·80	102	40·80	152	60·80	202	80·80	252	100·80	302	120·80	352	140·80	402	160·80	452	180·80
3	1·20	53	21·20	103	41·20	153	61·20	203	81·20	253	101·20	303	121·20	353	141·20	403	161·20	453	181·20
4	1·60	54	21·60	104	41·60	154	61·60	204	81·60	254	101·60	304	121·60	354	141·60	404	161·60	454	181·60
5	2·00	55	22·00	105	42·00	155	62·00	205	82·00	255	102·00	305	122·00	355	142·00	405	162·00	455	182·00
6	2·40	56	22·40	106	42·40	156	62·40	206	82·40	256	102·40	306	122·40	356	142·40	406	162·40	456	182·40
7	2·80	57	22·80	107	42·80	157	62·80	207	82·80	257	102·80	307	122·80	357	142·80	407	162·80	457	182·80
8	3·20	58	23·20	108	43·20	158	63·20	208	83·20	258	103·20	308	123·20	358	143·20	408	163·20	458	183·20
9	3·60	59	23·60	109	43·60	159	63·60	209	83·60	259	103·60	309	123·60	359	143·60	409	163·60	459	183·60
10	4·00	60	24·00	110	44·00	160	64·00	210	84·00	260	104·00	310	124·00	360	144·00	410	164·00	460	184·00
11	4·40	61	24·40	111	44·40	161	64·40	211	84·40	261	104·40	311	124·40	361	144·40	411	164·40	461	184·40
12	4·80	62	24·80	112	44·80	162	64·80	212	84·80	262	104·80	312	124·80	362	144·80	412	164·80	462	184·80
13	5·20	63	25·20	113	45·20	163	65·20	213	85·20	263	105·20	313	125·20	363	145·20	413	165·20	463	185·20
14	5·60	64	25·60	114	45·60	164	65·60	214	85·60	264	105·60	314	125·60	364	145·60	414	165·60	464	185·60
15	6·00	65	26·00	115	46·00	165	66·00	215	86·00	265	106·00	315	126·00	365	146·00	415	166·00	465	186·00
16	6·40	66	26·40	116	46·40	166	66·40	216	86·40	266	106·40	316	126·40	366	146·40	416	166·40	466	186·40
17	6·80	67	26·80	117	46·80	167	66·80	217	86·80	267	106·80	317	126·80	367	146·80	417	166·80	467	186·80
18	7·20	68	27·20	118	47·20	168	67·20	218	87·20	268	107·20	318	127·20	368	147·20	418	167·20	468	187·20
19	7·60	69	27·60	119	47·60	169	67·60	219	87·60	269	107·60	319	127·60	369	147·60	419	167·60	469	187·60
20	8·00	70	28·00	120	48·00	170	68·00	220	88·00	270	108·00	320	128·00	370	148·00	420	168·00	470	188·00
21	8·40	71	28·40	121	48·40	171	68·40	221	88·40	271	108·40	321	128·40	371	148·40	421	168·40	471	188·40
22	8·80	72	28·80	122	48·80	172	68·80	222	88·80	272	108·80	322	128·80	372	148·80	422	168·80	472	188·80
23	9·20	73	29·20	123	49·20	173	69·20	223	89·20	273	109·20	323	129·20	373	149·20	423	169·20	473	189·20
24	9·60	74	29·60	124	49·60	174	69·60	224	89·60	274	109·60	324	129·60	374	149·60	424	169·60	474	189·60
25	10·00	75	30·00	125	50·00	175	70·00	225	90·00	275	110·00	325	130·00	375	150·00	425	170·00	475	190·00
26	10·40	76	30·40	126	50·40	176	70·40	226	90·40	276	110·40	326	130·40	376	150·40	426	170·40	476	190·40
27	10·80	77	30·80	127	50·80	177	70·80	227	90·80	277	110·80	327	130·80	377	150·80	427	170·80	477	190·80
28	11·20	78	31·20	128	51·20	178	71·20	228	91·20	278	111·20	328	131·20	378	151·20	428	171·20	478	191·20
29	11·60	79	31·60	129	51·60	179	71·60	229	91·60	279	111·60	329	131·60	379	151·60	429	171·60	479	191·60
30	12·00	80	32·00	130	52·00	180	72·00	230	92·00	280	112·00	330	132·00	380	152·00	430	172·00	480	192·00
31	12·40	81	32·40	131	52·40	181	72·40	231	92·40	281	112·40	331	132·40	381	152·40	431	172·40	481	192·40
32	12·80	82	32·80	132	52·80	182	72·80	232	92·80	282	112·80	332	132·80	382	152·80	432	172·80	482	192·80
33	13·20	83	33·20	133	53·20	183	73·20	233	93·20	283	113·20	333	133·20	383	153·20	433	173·20	483	193·20
34	13·60	84	33·60	134	53·60	184	73·60	234	93·60	284	113·60	334	133·60	384	153·60	434	173·60	484	193·60
35	14·00	85	34·00	135	54·00	185	74·00	235	94·00	285	114·00	335	134·00	385	154·00	435	174·00	485	194·00
36	14·40	86	34·40	136	54·40	186	74·40	236	94·40	286	114·40	336	134·40	386	154·40	436	174·40	486	194·40
37	14·80	87	34·80	137	54·80	187	74·80	237	94·80	287	114·80	337	134·80	387	154·80	437	174·80	487	194·80
38	15·20	88	35·20	138	55·20	188	75·20	238	95·20	288	115·20	338	135·20	388	155·20	438	175·20	488	195·20
39	15·60	89	35·60	139	55·60	189	75·60	239	95·60	289	115·60	339	135·60	389	155·60	439	175·60	489	195·60
40	16·00	90	36·00	140	56·00	190	76·00	240	96·00	290	116·00	340	136·00	390	156·00	440	176·00	490	196·00
41	16·40	91	36·40	141	56·40	191	76·40	241	96·40	291	116·40	341	136·40	391	156·40	441	176·40	491	196·40
42	16·80	92	36·80	142	56·80	192	76·80	242	96·80	292	116·80	342	136·80	392	156·80	442	176·80	492	196·80
43	17·20	93	37·20	143	57·20	193	77·20	243	97·20	293	117·20	343	137·20	393	157·20	443	177·20	493	197·20
44	17·60	94	37·60	144	57·60	194	77·60	244	97·60	294	117·60	344	137·60	394	157·60	444	177·60	494	197·60
45	18·00	95	38·00	145	58·00	195	78·00	245	98·00	295	118·00	345	138·00	395	158·00	445	178·00	495	198·00
46	18·40	96	38·40	146	58·40	196	78·40	246	98·40	296	118·40	346	138·40	396	158·40	446	178·40	496	198·40
47	18·80	97	38·80	147	58·80	197	78·80	247	98·80	297	118·80	347	138·80	397	158·80	447	178·80	497	198·80
48	19·20	98	39·20	148	59·20	198	79·20	248	99·20	298	119·20	348	139·20	398	159·20	448	179·20	498	199·20
49	19·60	99	39·60	149	59·60	199	79·60	249	99·60	299	119·60	349	139·60	399	159·60	449	179·60	499	199·60
50	20·00	100	40·00	150	60·00	200	80·00	250	100·00	300	120·00	350	140·00	400	160·00	450	180·00	500	200·00

On		£1,000		£1,500		£2,000		£2,500		£3,000		£3,500		£4,000		£4,500		£5,000	
Tax		£400		£600		£800		£1,000		£1,200		£1,400		£1,600		£1,800		£2,000	

The Budget proposals are introduced by the Chancellor of the Exchequer in the House of Commons.

Note: Please remember that these proposals are subject to amendment during the passage of the Finance Bill through Parliament.

Tax rates and allowances

	2011–12 (£)	2012–13 (£)
Personal allowance	7,475	8,105
Income limit for personal allowance (reduces by £1 for every £2 where income is over £100, 000, irrespective of age)	100,000	100,000
Aged 65 or over in year of assessment	9,940	10,500
Aged 75 or over in year of assessment	10,090	10,660
Age allowance income limit	24,000	25,400
Minimum where limit exceeded	7,475	8,105
Married couple's allowance (10% relief)		
Either spouse aged 75 or over in year of assessment	7,295	7,705
Age allowance income limit	24,000	25,400
Minimum where limit exceeded	2,800	2,960
Blind person's allowance	1,980	2,100

Income tax rates

	2011–12 (£)	2012–13 (£)
Starting rate	10%	10%
On taxable income up to	2,560*	2,710*

*10% starting rate applies to savings income only. If non-savings income is above this limit then the 10% starting rate for savings does not apply.

	2011–12 (£)	2012–13 (£)
Basic rate	20%	20%
On taxable income up to	35,000	34,370
Higher rate	40%	40%
On taxable income over	35,000	34,370
Additional higher rate	50%	50%
On taxable income over	150,000	150,000
Lower rate on dividend income	10%	10%
Higher rate on dividend income	32.5%	32.5%
Additional higher rate	42.5%	42.5%

Company Taxation

	FY2011	FY2012
Corporation tax rates		
Main rate	26%	24%
Companies with small profits	20%	20%
– 20% rate limit	£300,000	£300,000
– marginal relief limit	£1,500,000	£1,500,000
– marginal rate	27.5%	25%

Capital gains

Rates	
–Individuals	18%/28%*
–Trustees and personal representatives	28%

–Entrepreneurs' relief flat rate	10%
General exemption limit	£10,600

*Chargeable gains are aggregated with taxable income and to the extent that the aggregate falls above the income tax basic rate threshold, CGT is charged at 28%(taking the chargeable gains as being the highest part of that aggregate). If the aggregate falls below the threshold, the CGT rate will be 18%.

Inheritance Tax

Threshold (year from 6/4/2012)	325,000
Death rate	40%

VAT

Standard rate	20%
Registration threshold from 1 April 2012	£77,000

(previously £73,000 from 1 April 2011)

National Insurance

Class 1 Contributions

Not contracted out

The employee contribution is 12% of earnings between £146 and £817 pw plus 2% on earnings over £817 pw.

The employer contribution is 13.8% of all earnings in excess of the first £144 pw

Contracted out

The 'not contracted out' rates for employees are reduced on the band of earnings from £146 pw to £817 pw by 1.6%. For employers, they are reduced on the band of earnings from £144 pw to £817 pw by 3.4% for employees in salary-related schemes or 1.4% for employees in money purchase schemes. In addition, there is an employee rebate of 1.6% and an employer rebate of 3.4% or 1.4% as appropriate on earnings from £107 (£102 for 2011/12) pw up to £144/£146 pw.

Class 1A and 1B contributions	13.8%	13.8%
Class 2 contributions		
Flat weekly rate	£2.50	£2.65
Exemption limit	£5,315	£5,595
Class 3 contributions		
Flat weekly rate	£12.60	£13.25
Class 4 contributions		

9% on profits between £7,605 (£7,225) and £42,475 (£42,475) plus

2% on profits over £42,475 (£42,475)

Personal taxes, national insurance and capital gains tax

Income tax rates

For 2013/14 the basic rate of income tax will be 20%, the higher rate will be 40%, and the additional rate will be 45%. The dividend additional rate will be 37.5%, the trust rate will be 45% and the dividend trust rate will be 37.5%.

For 2013/14 the charge on benefits paid to non-individuals under an employer-financed retirement benefits scheme will reduce from 50% to 45%. Where capital sums are deemed to be income of a settlor, the rate of tax taken as paid by the trustees will also reduce from 50% to 45%.

Income tax personal allowance for those aged under 65, basic rate limit and upper earnings limit for 2013/14

From April 2013, the personal allowance will rise to £9,205 (£8,105 for 2012/13). The basic rate limit will be reduced to £32,245 (£34,370 for 2012/13).

The NIC Upper Earnings Limit (UEL) and Upper Profits Limit (UPL) will continue to be aligned with the level of the higher rate threshold (the total of the personal allowance and the basic rate limit) by separate regulations.

Changes to the higher personal allowances for people aged 65 to 74 and aged 75 and over

From 2013/14, the availability of the 'age-related' income tax personal allowances will be restricted. The allowance of £10,500 for 2012/13, available to people aged 65 to 74, will be restricted to people born after 5 April 1938 but before 6 April 1948. The allowance of £10,660 for 2012/13, available to people aged 75 and over, will be restricted to people born before 6 April 1938. From 2013/14, the amounts of these allowances will not be increased. From 2013/14, people born after 5 April 1948 will be entitled to the basic personal allowance of £9,205.

Venture capital reliefs

Enterprise investment scheme (EIS) and venture capital trusts (VCTs): simplification

The EIS rules defining when a person is connected to a company through an interest in its capital are to be amended, and the definition of shares which qualify for relief is to be widened. In addition, the current £500 minimum investment limit is to be removed. These changes apply to shares issued on or after 6 April 2012. Finance Bill 2012 will contain legislation to:

- disregard loan capital for the purposes of the limit on the proportion of a company's capital which an investor can hold without being treated as 'connected'; and
- allow shares to carry a preferential right to dividends providing their amount and the date that they are payable is not dependent on a decision of the company, the holder or anyone else, and providing that the dividends are not cumulative.

The £1 million limit on investment by a VCT in a single company (except for companies in a partnership or a joint venture) is to be removed. This change applies to shares issued on or after 1 April 2012.

Enterprise investment scheme (EIS) and venture capital trusts (VCTs): increases to thresholds

Subject to state aid approval, legislation will be introduced in Finance Bill 2012 to increase:

- the thresholds for the maximum size of qualifying company for both EIS and VCTs; and
- the maximum annual amount that can be invested in an individual company under all the venture capital schemes.

Legislation will be introduced in Finance Bill 2012 to increase:

- the employee limit to fewer than 250 employees;
- the size threshold to gross assets of no more than £15 million before investment and £16 million after; and
- the maximum annual amount that can be invested in an individual company, to £5 million.

Legislation will also restrict to £5 million in total the amount of investment which a company may receive in a 12-month period from any state-aided risk capital measure, including EIS and VCT.

Subject to state aid approval these changes will apply to shares in investee companies that are issued on or after 6 April 2012.

Legislation will also increase the annual amount that an individual can invest under the EIS to £1million. This has already received state aid approval and will apply to the tax year 2012/13 and subsequent years.

Enterprise management incentives (EMIs)

Qualifying businesses can grant tax-advantaged share options to their employees under EMIs. The limit on the value of shares over which options may be held by an employee under EMI will be increased from its current level of £120,000 to £250,000. The measure will have effect in respect of EMI options granted on or after the date set by statutory instrument. The Government's intention is to implement the measure as soon as possible, subject to state aid approval.

Seed enterprise investment scheme

As announced in the Autumn Statement 2011, from 6 April 2012, investors will be able to obtain tax relief on qualifying investments into seed enterprise investment schemes (SEIS). The new scheme focuses on smaller, early stage companies carrying on, or preparing to carry on, a new business in a qualifying trade. The scheme will make available tax relief to investors who subscribe for shares and have a stake of less than 30% in the company. In addition, for the first year of the new scheme, gains realised on the disposal of assets in 2012/13 that are invested through SEIS in the same year will be exempt from capital gains tax. Broadly, the scheme will:

- apply to companies with 25 or fewer employees and assets of up to £200,000;
- give income tax relief worth 50% of the amount invested to individual investors with a stake of less than 30% in such companies, including directors who invest in their companies;
- apply to subscriptions for shares, using the same definition of eligible shares as EIS;
- apply to an annual amount of investment of £100,000 per investor, with unused annual amounts able to be carried back to the previous year, as under EIS;

- provide for relief within an overall tax favoured investment limit of £150,000 for the company. This will be a cumulative limit, not an annual limit;
- provide for an exemption from CGT on gains on shares within the scope of the SEIS; and
- provide for an exemption from CGT on gains realised from disposals of assets in 2012/13, where the gains are reinvested through the new SEIS in the same year.

Following consultation on the original announcement, the 2012 Budget confirmed that certain changes have been made to the proposed legislation to allow companies to:
- qualify if they have subsidiaries;
- determine eligibility by reference to the age of any trade rather than to the age of the company;
- remove reference to the holdings of other entities in calculating asset and employee tests;
- allow previous (but not current) employees to qualify; and
- allow directors who have qualified under SEIS to continue to qualify under EIS, subject to time limits.

Enterprise investment scheme (EIS) and venture capital trusts (VCTs): better focus

Changes to EIS and VCTs aim to focus the schemes better on higher risk activities, preventing tax relief being provided for investment in companies or activities outside the purpose of the schemes and so helping smaller, higher-risk UK companies to obtain finance.

Legislation will be introduced in Finance Bill 2012 to:
- introduce a new disqualifying purpose test. The test will disqualify shares which are issued subject to arrangements whose main purpose is to generate access to the reliefs in circumstances where either the benefit of the investment is passed to another party to the arrangements, or the business activities would otherwise be carried on by another party. For both EIS and VCTs the new test applies to shares in underlying investee companies issued on or after 6 April 2012;
- amend the definition of qualifying business activity to exclude acquiring existing shares in another company. The exclusion applies for EIS, to shares issued on or after 6 April

2012 and for VCTs, to money invested in a VCT on or after that date; and

- provide that activity comprising receipt of feed in tariffs (FiTs) or similar subsidies will not generally be a qualifying activity. There are a number of exceptions to this. Electricity generated by anaerobic digestion or hydro power, and projects operated by community interest companies, co-operative societies, community benefit societies or Northern Ireland industrial and provident societies will not be affected. For both EIS and VCTs, the exclusion applies to all shares in underlying investee companies issued on or after 6 April 2012. The exclusion also applies to shares issued between 23 March 2011 and 6 April 2012 where the investee company had not commenced subsidised electricity generation before 6 April 2012.

Child benefit: income tax charge for those on higher income

A new income tax charge will be applied to taxpayers whose income exceeds £50,000 in a tax year and who are in receipt of Child Benefit, and to taxpayers whose income exceeds £50,000 and whose partner is in receipt of Child Benefit. In the event that both partners have an income that exceeds £50,000, the charge will apply only to the partner with the highest income. For taxpayers with income between £50,000 and £60,000, the amount of the charge will be a proportion of the Child Benefit received. For taxpayers with income above £60,000, the amount of the charge will equal the amount of Child Benefit received.

The amount of Child Benefit payable will be unaffected by the new tax charge. This measure takes effect from 7 January 2013.

Reform of the taxation of non-domiciled individuals

A higher annual charge of £50,000 (previously £30,000) for those non-domiciles who claim the remittance basis in a tax year, and have been resident in at least 12 of the previous 14 tax years, applies from 6 April 2012.

From 6 April 2012 non-domiciles may remit their overseas income or capital gains to the UK tax-free, where they do so for the purposes of making a 'qualifying investment'. A 'qualifying investment' is an investment in unlisted companies, or those listed on exchange regulated markets, which carry out trading activity on a commercial basis or undertake the development or letting of commercial property. There will be specific anti-avoidance provisions to ensure the investment is made on proper commercial terms.

The nominated income rules are amended to allow individuals to remit up to £10 of overseas income or capital gains which they have nominated for the purposes of the annual remittance basis charge, without being taxed on that remittance and without becoming subject to the identification rules. This applies both for the purposes of the former £30,000 charge, and for the new increased £50,000 charge.

A new provision will remove the tax charge that arises where exempt property remitted to the UK ceases to be exempt property as a result of being sold in the UK. This exemption will apply to all exempt property and will not be restricted to any particular class of asset or sector of the economy. There will be specific anti-avoidance provisions requiring the vendor to send the sale proceeds offshore in order to benefit from the exemption.

Capital gains tax

Annual exempt amount

The capital gains tax (CGT) annual exempt amount for 2012/13 is £10,600 (unchanged from 2011/12). From 2013/14 the annual exemption will rise each year in line with the consumer prices index (CPI) instead of the retail prices index (RPI), subject to override if Parliament determines a different amount should apply.

Single payment scheme and CGT roll-over relief

A new measure will preserve the availability of roll-over relief in relation to rights to single payment scheme (SPS) payments following changes to the EU scheme. The revisions in this measure will be retrospective and have effect on or after 1 January 2009.

Foreign currency bank accounts

Capital gains arising on withdrawals of money in foreign currency bank accounts will not be liable to capital gains tax (CGT), and capital losses will not be allowable losses. Broadly, this measure will increase simplicity in the tax system by reducing administrative burdens in certain cases, by removing foreign currency bank accounts (FCBAs) from the scope of CGT. The measure has effect for withdrawals of money from FCBAs on or after 6 April 2012.

Inheritance tax nil rate band: switch to consumer prices index

Legislation will be introduced in Finance Bill 2012 to provide for the inheritance tax nil rate band to rise in line with the consumer prices index (CPI) instead of the retail prices index (RPI) from 6 April 2015. Automatic indexation using the CPI will still be subject to override if Parliament determines a different amount should apply.

Tax exemptions: international military headquarters, EU forces, etc

A change to the current rules will mean that members of EU forces and their civilian staff will receive the tax privileges to which they are entitled under the EU Status of Forces Agreement. These privileges are the same as already apply to visiting North Atlantic Treaty Organisation (NATO) forces. The measure will have effect on and after the date that Finance Bill 2012 receives Royal Assent.

Income tax exemption: armed forces continuity of education allowance

Payments of continuity of education allowance (CEA) to service personnel and payments in respect of the children of deceased service personnel will be exempt from income tax. The CEA is currently liable to tax when paid to recipients based in the UK but the tax is paid by the Ministry of Defence on behalf of CEA recipients. The financial impact of the measure will be neutral for service personnel and their families but the measure will simplify administration of the allowance. The measure will have effect for payments made on and after 6 April 2012.

Company car tax rates

For 2014/15 the appropriate percentage of the list price subject to tax will be increased by one percentage point for cars emitting more than 75g of carbon dioxide per kilometre, to a maximum of 35%. In both 2015/16 and 2016/17, the appropriate percentages of the list price subject to tax will increase by two percentage points, to a maximum of 37%.

In addition, new European standards which come into force in September 2015 will require diesel cars to have the same air quality emissions as petrol cars. The diesel supplement will therefore be removed in April 2016.

Company car tax: security enhanced cars

A change to the existing company car taxation rules will exclude certain passive security enhancements from being treated as accessories for the purpose of calculating the cash equivalent of the benefit of a company car made available for private use. The change will have effect for relevant benefits provided on or after 6 April 2011.

Security enhancements do not currently fall within any of the four categories of excluded accessory set out in ITEPA 2003, s 125. In particular, they are not equipment necessarily provided for use in the performance of the duties of the employment. This measure will treat certain security enhancements as excluded accessories. The particular enhancements are:

- armour designed to protect the car's occupants from explosions or gunfire;
- bullet-resistant glass;
- any modifications to the car's fuel tank designed to protect the tank's contents from explosions or gunfire (including by making the tank self-sealing); and
- any modification made to the car in consequence of anything which is a relevant security feature by virtue of the preceding three examples.

The relief will be confined to those individuals who can demonstrate that the nature of their employment creates a threat to their personal security.

Summary of Budget Proposals 21 March 2012

Company car fuel benefit charge

The multiplier used to calculate the cash equivalent of the benefit of free fuel provided to employees is increased from £18,800 to £20,200 for the tax year 2012/13. There is a further commitment to increase the multiplier by 2% above the rate of inflation (RPI) for the tax year 2013/14 which will be legislated by Order in the autumn, following confirmation of the September 2012 inflation figure. As a result of this change the fuel benefit charge will increase for fuel provided for all cars apart from zero emissions cars.

Taxation of non-residents: champions league final 2013

With effect from Royal Assent to Finance Bill 2012, there will be an exemption from UK taxation for non-resident footballers and team officials for money earned in relation to the champions league final 2013, which is to be held in the UK. The exemption has been put in place to satisfy the UEFA's requirement that countries hosting the champions league final do not levy domestic tax on non-resident players and team officials involved in the final.

Qualifying time deposits: deduction of tax at source

From 6 April 2012, any qualifying time deposits (QTD) provider who operates the tax deduction scheme for interest (TDSI) will be required to deduct sums representing income tax at the basic rate from interest, dividends or similar payments they make in respect of QTD investments opened or made after this date.

This measure will align tax collection arrangements for QTDs with those already in operation for many comparable savings or investment products.

Resettlement payments made to members of parliament

From 1 April 2012 the MPs' Expenses Scheme administered by the Independent Parliamentary Standards Authority (IPSA) will include provision for a resettlement payment to any MP who involuntarily leaves office on or after that date. This measure introduces an income tax exemption for such payments (subject to a £30,000 limit). The aim of this measure is to ensure that resettlement payments made by IPSA are treated in the same way as resettlement grants previously paid under the House of Commons Members' Allowances Scheme, similar grants payable to members of the devolved administrations, and termination payments received by other employees and office holders.

Pensions tax

Basic state pension

From 6 April 2012 the basic state pension will increase by £5.30 per week from £102.15 to £107.45. However, the Government remains committed to the introduction of replacing the basic state pension and S2P by a single pension currently expected to be £140 per week to take everyone out of means tested benefits. Consultation on this will take place in the summer 2012.

The Government has accepted the need to link state pension age to future changes in life expectancy and will consult on this in summer 2012 as well.

Annual allowance

Technical amendments to the legislation in the Finance Act 2011 will be made by regulation to ensure that the rules surrounding scheme pays and deferred members work as intended in the application of the annual allowance at a level of £50,000 from 6 April 2011.

Lifetime allowance

The Chancellor confirmed that there would be no change to the proposed reduction in the level of the lifetime allowance from £1.8 million to £1.5 million from 6 April 2012. A regulation-making power will be included in the Finance Bill 2013 to ensure that the rules surrounding fixed protection work as intended.

Asset-backed pension contributions

The Chancellor confirmed that the change in the tax rules in relation to employer asset-backed pension contributions applies from 29 November 2011. The subsequent change, to limit the circumstances in which up-front relief can be given to asset-backed arrangements, remains in place from 22 February 2012. Additional changes to existing legislation are contained in Finance Bill 2012, Schedule 1, which includes transitional provision.

Commutation of small personal pension funds

The Chancellor confirmed that the existing pension tax commutation rules will be extended to allow individuals aged 60 and over to commute pension funds of £2,000 or less held in personal pensions into a lump sum. The change was previously announced in the Autumn Statement 2011 and applies regardless of other pension savings, subject to a maximum of two commutations in a lifetime. Regulations have now been made (the Registered Pension Schemes (Authorised Payments) (Amendment) Regulation 2012 (SI 2012/522)) and come into force on the 6 April 2012.

Contracting-out

The pensions' tax legislation is to be amended to remove the references which apply to tax relief on employee contracted-out contributions to defined contribution schemes. Contracting-out for such schemes will be abolished under DWP legislation from 6 April 2012. The tax changes will be contained in the Finance Bill 2013.

Qualifying recognised overseas pension schemes (QROPS)

Following a consultation on draft amendments to secondary legislation regarding QROPS, the Government confirmed their support for the proposed changes included in new regulations (the Registered Pension Schemes and Overseas Pension Schemes (Miscellaneous Amendments) Regulations 2012 (SI 2012/884)). These have now been made and come into force from 6 April 2012, amending existing secondary legislation with the objectives of:

- introducing a new requirement to qualify as QROPS that any tax exemption available to non-residents of a jurisdiction must also be available to residents;
- introducing new and shorter-timescale information requirements on a QROPS and UK registered pension schemes making a transfer to a QROPS;

- extending the reporting period from up to five years' of non-residency to the later of five years' of non-residency and 10 years from the date of transfer from a UK pension scheme.

A number of jurisdictions already have new legislation ready to be applied from 6 April 2012 in anticipation of today's regulations.

Additional reporting requirements are included in the Finance Bill 2012 and the Government has also announced that it will introduce legislation in the Finance Bill 2013 to exclude schemes from being QROPS in any jurisdictions that makes legislation or otherwise creates or uses a pension scheme to provide tax advantages that are not intended to be available under QROPS rules.

Unfunded workplace pension arrangements

The Government is to continue monitoring the use of unfunded pension arrangements to ensure that they are not used to circumnavigate the restriction on pensions' tax relief and the disguised remuneration rules which are contained in the Finance Act 2011.

Contributions paid to spouses or family members

Provision will be made in the Finance Bill 2013 to ensure that any payment of employer contributions into a registered pension scheme for an employee's spouse or family member, as part of their employee's flexible remuneration package, cannot be used to mitigate tax and national insurance contributions by the employer or employee.

Bridging pensions

The legislation and tax rules which apply to the payment of bridging pensions to members prior to attaining state pension age will be revised to accommodate the forthcoming changes to state pension age under DWP legislation. The statutory change will be contained in the Finance Bill 2013.

Miscellaneous matters affecting overseas pension arrangements

Other miscellaneous changes announced may affect overseas pension arrangements in relation to:

- an extension of the capital gains tax regime from 2013 to gains on the disposal of UK residential property (and shares or interests in such property) by non-resident 'non-natural persons';
- income on transfers of assets abroad sheltered in 'overseas envelopes';
- extension of stamp duty land tax (SDLT) to overseas 'corporate envelopes' in respect future purchase of UK residential property over £2 million, at a rate of 15%;
- consultation on an SDLT claw-back on such properties already transferred to overseas 'corporate envelopes'.

Charities and philanthropy

Gifts of pre-eminent objects

The acceptance in lieu (AIL) scheme allows taxpayers to offer items of cultural or historical importance for public ownership in settlement of inheritance tax. As from 1 April 2012 a similar scheme will run in parallel with the existing AIL scheme such that the donor will receive a fixed tax reduction of 30% of the item's agreed value of income or capital gains tax liabilities for individuals and 20% for corporation tax. The total tax reductions under the new scheme together with taxes offset under the AIL scheme, will be restricted to an increased annual limit of £30 million per year. Donors will be able to spread the tax reduction forward across a period of up to five years starting with the tax year in which the item is offered.

The item must be 'pre-eminent' such that it is of particular national, scientific, historic or artistic significance to include pre-existing works of art but not land and buildings, which are subject to a separate relief.

Gifts are to be made by an 'offer and acceptance' process between the donor and Government on behalf of the nation; meaning that no gifts can be made to specific museums or galleries thus donors will not be able to gift an item to a charity for resale.

IHT – reduced rate for estates leaving 10% or more to charity

IHT is charged at a flat rate of 40% on the net chargeable value of an estate, after reliefs, exemptions and the available nil-rate band have been deducted. As from 6 April 2012 that rate will be reduced to 36% if at least 10% of the estate is left to charity.

The reduced rate will apply automatically if the amount gifted exceeds the 10% test but if less, the full 40% rate will be levied. Personal representatives will be able to elect for the reduced rate not to apply if, for example, the benefit obtained from applying the reduced rate is likely to be minimal and/or they do not wish to incur additional costs of valuing items.

'In-year' repayments of tax to charities

To aid cash flow certain charities make claims for repayment of tax 'in-year' which legally should be made at the end of the tax year on submission of the annual tax return. This measure places this 'extra statutory concession' on a statutory footing thus bringing the treatment of such claims in line with the rules that currently apply to gift aid.

Community amateur sports clubs (CASCs): registration and gift aid

As a concession HMRC have allowed clubs run on an amateur basis providing facilities for and promotion of participation in eligible sports for the local community to be exempt from tax and to make gift aid tax claims. These sections place the concession on a statutory basis applying with retrospective effect as from 1 April 2010 in relation to gift aid receipts and 6 April 2010 in relation to gift aid claims. CASCs will no longer need to amend their constitutions to retain their status as previously the tax relief was available only to companies.

Corporate taxes

Corporation tax: main rate

The main rate of corporation tax will be reduced in Finance Bill 2012 (for all non-ring fence profits) to 24% for the financial year commencing 1 April 2012, and to 23% for the financial year commencing 1 April 2013. The corporation tax main rate will be further reduced (by legislation in Finance Bill 2013) to 22% for the financial year commencing 1 April 2014.

Grouping rules

Under current legislation, the holders of loans which carry a right of conversion into further loans or into shares are considered part of the equity capital of the issuing company, with a consequent impact on the availability of tax reliefs and exemptions reliant on a group relationship (such as the group relief rules and capital gains groups). Within the financial sector it is becoming more common to issue loans with a right to conversion into shares of listed companies that are not connected with the lender, as an alternative to repayment of the loan. This is an attractive option with the current low interest rates, as it can improve the return to the lender if the underlying shares have over-performed.

However, as these loans carry a right of conversion into shares they are technically equity instruments for tax purposes and can therefore be unattractive from a tax grouping perspective.

Legislation will be introduced in Finance Bill 2012 so that loans that carry rights of conversion into an unconnected company listed on a recognised stock exchange are to be treated as normal commercial loans.

The legislation will have effect for transactions where the relevant day falls on or after 21 March 2012.

Controlled foreign companies

A controlled foreign company (CFC) is an overseas company controlled by UK resident companies that pays tax at a lower rate than it would have done if it were a UK resident company. The CFC rules apply if the rate of tax of the CFC is less than three quarters of the UK corporation tax rate applied to the company's profits, measured using UK tax rules.

The CFC provisions are directed at companies which artificially divert UK profits to low tax territories or other favourable overseas tax regimes to reduce their UK tax liabilities. The leg-islation has been under review for several years now and we will have a completely new CFC code in Finance Act 2012, the intention being that the new rules will apply in respect of company accounting periods starting on or after 1 January 2013.

The draft legislation published in December 2011 comprised 60 pages of complex rules.

A redrafted 'gateway' provision was issued in March 2012. The overall intention of the gateway is to ensure that the CFC legislation only applies to business profits that are artificially diverted from the UK, so the majority of controlled foreign companies should be filtered out at this stage by a series of relatively straightforward and easy to apply tests. A company will not be a CFC for general business (i.e. non-financial) profits so long as it passes one of the following four tests:

- The company does not have any UK managed assets or any UK managed risks at any time during the accounting period.
- The company has the capability to carry on its business in a commercially effective way if any UK management of its assets or risks were, instead, borne by the company itself or otherwise no longer managed in the UK.
- The arrangements through which a foreign subsidiary derives its profits do not have a main purpose of achieving a reduction in the UK tax charge. This condition will usually be met where the arrangements have a commercial purpose and would probably have been entered into without the tax advantages.
- The company only has property business profits or non-trading finance profits.

As well as the gateway, the intention of the legislation is that there be 'safe harbours' for general commercial business, incidental finance income and certain sector-specific categories. There will also be general exemptions for low profits and for excluded territories.

There are also rules relating to exempt foreign branches and a deferred commencement provision where CFCs are acquired.

Notwithstanding the promised commencement date, many commentators are concerned that the current rules are still too complex and difficult to operate and that the legislation may not be ready in time for a 1 January 2013 commencement.

Summary of Budget Proposals 21 March 2012

Patent box

The long promised patent box legislation will be introduced in Finance Act 2012 and will have effect in relation to profits made on or after 1 April 2013. This will allow companies to apply a 10% rate of corporation tax to profits attributable to qualifying intellectual property, which includes patents granted by the UK Intellectual Property Office and the European Patent Office. The regime will also be extended to patents granted by other EU countries with 'similar examination and patentability criteria as the UK' (although it is not entirely clear whether such a restriction would survive a challenge under EU anti-discrimination rules). A list of qualifying patent jurisdictions will be published as secondary legislation in 2012.

The favourable tax rate will also apply to supplementary protection certificates, regulatory data protection and plant variety rights and will apply to existing intellectual property as well as new. Where a company acquires intellectual property, the 10% rate applies to profits where the group has further developed the intellectual property or the product incorporating it.

The 10% corporation tax rate will apply subject to the full rate of corporation tax being charged on a 10% routine return on certain costs and on any part of the profits attributable to marketing intangibles. For smaller claims, companies will be able to choose a simpler calculation that avoids the need to value the brand. This applies for companies selling patented products or licensing their patents. Where companies use intellectual property to perform processes or provide services, they can benefit from the patent box up to the level of an arm's-length royalty for the use of the qualifying intellectual property.

Once again, the legislation is lengthy, comprising 37 pages in draft. This is a major concern, as it is likely that smaller companies, to whom this new regime might be very helpful, would be put off making claims due to the length and complexity of the legislation and, therefore, the likely costs of a claim.

Research and development tax relief

The rules for research and development tax relief will be substantially more generous from 1 April 2012. For small or medium enterprises (SMEs) the improvements are:

- The enhanced deduction will be 125% so that the total relief is 225% of the actual expenditure. This will have effect for expenditure on or after 1 April 2012.
- The rule limiting the payable tax credit to a company's pay as you earn/NIC liability will be removed for accounting periods ending on or after 1 April 2012.
- For SMEs and large companies the requirement for minimum expenditure of £10,000 a year will be removed for accounting periods ending on or after 1 April 2012.
- For SMEs and large companies the definition of an 'externally provided worker' will be widened for expenditure on or after 1 April 2012.

In order to remain within state aid limits, the rate of payable tax credit for SMEs will be reduced to 11% and the vaccine research relief (VRR) for SME companies will be withdrawn for expenditure on or after 1 April 2012. This latter point is unlikely to be of any major significance, as anecdotal evidence is that the VRR has barely been used by SMEs.

The existing definition of a company as a going concern will also be clarified in order to ensure that companies in administration or liquidation are excluded from relief. This 'clarification' will apply to claims made on or after 1 April 2012.

Capital allowances

Enterprises zones

New enterprise zones have been announced and there will be 100% first year allowances for expenditure incurred by trading companies on qualifying plant or machinery between 1 April 2012 and 31 March 2017. The plant and machinery must be for use primarily in designated assisted areas within enterprise zones.

Enterprise zones are designed to encourage new investment, so qualifying expenditure must be on unused plant and machinery, not second hand, and must actually be an investment and not merely replacement expenditure for old plant and machinery.

There are also a number of restrictions for EU purposes, so that the allowances would not be available to certain firms in financial difficulty, or companies involved in the fisheries, aquaculture, coal, steel, shipbuilding, synthetic fibres, agricultural products, road freight and air transport sectors.

Enhanced capital allowances

Certain items of plant and machinery qualify for a 100% rate of capital allowances on the basis of being energy or water efficient or improving water quality. The Energy Technology Criteria List and Water Technology Criteria List, reviewed annually by DECC and DEFRA, are to be amended to include Heat Pump Driven Air curtains and remove Combustion Trim Controls, Energy Saving Controls for Desiccant Air Dryers and Sequence Controls.

The criteria for certain other technologies and for toilets, showers, taps and industrial washing machines in the water efficient scheme will also be tightened, and minor changes will be made to the existing criteria of both schemes.

The changes to the schemes will have effect on and after a date to be appointed by Treasury Order to be made prior to the summer 2012 Parliamentary recess.

Capital allowances: feed-in tariffs

Certain plant or machinery generates electricity or heat, or produces bio-gas or bio-fuel, and attracts feed-in tariffs or renewable heat incentives.

Some of this plant and machinery would also qualify for the 100% enhanced capital allowances for expenditure on energy saving plant and machinery. This represents a duplication of Government policy, so for expenditure from 1 April 2012 (for corporation tax), or 6 April 2012 (for income tax), such plant and machinery will no longer qualify for enhanced capital allowances.

For similar reasons, from 1 or 6 April 2012, expenditure on solar panels will be deemed to qualify only for special rate capital allowances at 8% a year on a writing down basis, rather than the main rate of 18%.

Capital allowances: fixtures

Following a consultation process, new rules for the pooling of qualifying fixtures have been proposed. These are intended to prevent late claims being made for capital allowances on fixtures on property acquired many years before, when the position of the vendor can no longer be verified. This meant that HMRC could not be sure that the total allowances in respect of fixtures were being restricted to the initial cost of those fixtures, as the allowances that had been claimed by previous owners could not be verified.

Under the new rules a purchaser of fixtures will only be able to claim capital allowances if the previous expenditure on those fixtures had been pooled by the vendor before sale and the vendor and purchaser have agreed the value of the fixtures at the date of transfer. This agreement must be made within two years of the date of transfer and would normally be done by a joint election for the sale price to be attributed to the fixtures, capped at the original cost to the seller. If they cannot reach agreement within two years, the matter can be referred to the First-tier Tribunal for a determination. Either party will be able to invoke this facility. The referral to the Tribunal must be made within the two years following a transfer.

A purchaser of fixtures may also be able to claim capital allowances where, exceptionally, a vendor provides a statement of the disposal value he has brought into account for the fixtures in the past (for example, if he had ceased business some time before). Again, this statement must be provided within two years of the later sale of the property.

This measure will apply to expenditure on or after 1 April 2012 for corporation tax purposes or 6 April 2012 for income tax purposes.

Improvements to real estate investment trust (REIT) regime

In order to support expansion of the property sector and stimulate the construction industry, and following consultation, a number of improvements have been made to REITs, the tax advantaged vehicle for property investment. The improvements include removal of certain barriers to entry and relaxing some of the conditions that REITs must satisfy.

The improvements to barriers to entry include:
- A company joining the REIT regime will no longer have to pay a 2% entry charge based on the value of assets involved in the property rental business.

- The current requirement that REITs be listed on a recognised stock exchange will be relaxed, so that they can also be listed on other trading platforms such as AIM and foreign equivalents.
- Currently, a REIT must have diverse ownership and cannot be a close company (i.e. controlled by five or fewer persons or any number of shareholder directors). Instead, a REIT will be permitted to remain close for a certain amount of time after listing. Furthermore, certain types of institutional investor will be permitted without the REIT being a close company.

The improvements to the conditions for qualification as a REIT include:

- Currently, a REIT must be primarily a property investment company such that the profits and assets of the property rental business must constitute 75% or more of the total profit or assets. This rule is being relaxed to allow cash to be added to the assets of the property rental business.
- The amount of borrowing by a REIT is restricted by taxing excessive financing costs, and this rule is being relaxed by restricting financing costs only to interest. The tax charge on excessive interest will also be restricted to a proportion of the property profits.
- There are some other minor changes to the rules.

The new rules will apply to companies that enter the regime on or after the date of Royal Assent, insofar as they relate to the barriers to entry. The other measures will have effect for REITs generally on or after the date of Royal Assent to Finance Bill 2012.

Tax transparent investment fund

This legislates for the setting up of a special type of authorised 'mutual' fund which meets the criteria laid down by the European Union. It is relevant for UK authorised unit trusts, Open Ended Investment Companies (OEICs), pension funds and insurance companies.

Bank levy: 2013 rate change

Originally proposed by the International Monetary Fund (IMF) as a type of insurance scheme, the bank levy is an annual tax on the value of all debts held by the UK banks. For periods falling wholly or partly after 1 January 2013, the rate applying to chargeable equity and long-term chargeable liabilities will be increased from 0.044% to 0.0525% and the rate for short-term chargeable liabilities will be increased from 0.088% to 0.105%. An 'Amendments' section is included to bring specific foreign banking groups operating in the UK within the bank levy regime.

Solvency II and the taxation of life insurance companies

This places into UK law the EU Solvency Directive II ('the Directive') which most European insurers are obliged to implement within the next two years.

The taxation of UK life insurance companies is currently based on the figures declared on the regulatory returns required to be made annually to the Financial Services Authority (FSA). The Directive establishes a new regulatory framework such that, from 1 January 2013, FSA returns will no longer exist. The need to implement the Directive has allowed the opportunity to review the method by which life companies' taxable profits are computed. The most fundamental change is the move to an accounts basis in line with general tax rules for all companies. The changes under the new regime include bringing life companies within the same rules on loan relationships and intangible fixed assets which apply to companies generally.

General insurance: claims equalisation reserves

This is also included as a result of needing to enforce the EU Solvency Directive II. Under the Directive a revised set of EU-wide capital requirements and risk management standards replace the current solvency requirements. Claims equalisation reserves are reserves built up by UK general insurance companies and Lloyd's members that will no longer be required and, as such, this measure seeks to tax the reserves over a six-year transitional period commencing from the date that the Directive solvency requirements come into force.

This tax treatment is subject to an election which may be made in any year during the transitional period (including year one) to tax the full amount (as reduced by any previous one-sixth releases) of any built-up reserve.

Lloyd's: stop-loss insurance

Stop-loss insurance is a form of re-insurance contract used by members of Lloyd's. This change amends the basis of deduction of premiums such that payments are accounted for in the year that the profits are made rather than, as currently, the year in which the expense is incurred.

Distributions of assets

Following a number of changes to the distributions legislation, mainly in the context of the tax treatment of distributions received by UK resident companies, further uncertainties were identified in relation to the treatment of distributions of assets in kind. Such a transfer in kind was treated as not being a distribution where the distributing company and the recipient company were both UK resident and either one was a 51% subsidiary of the other, or both were 51% subsidiaries of a third UK company or, alternatively, if the companies were not under common control and neither was a 51% subsidiary of a non-UK resident company. As a result, the tax treatment of distributions of assets in kind depended on the residence of the companies involved. There was no reason for this difference, which related to the advance corporation tax regime, abolished in 1998.

Where such a transfer of assets did not constitute a distribution, it was also not treated as a distribution received by the recipient and could, therefore, constitute a capital distribution carrying a charge to corporation tax on chargeable gains. Under the revised rule, a distribution of assets will be treated as a distribution for the purposes of the Corporation Tax Acts. For the recipient company, in the majority of cases, this will be exempt income under the relevant provisions of CTA 2009, Pt 9A and will also not constitute a capital distribution.

This measure will apply for transfers of assets and liabilities made on or after the date of Royal Assent to Finance Bill 2012.

The treatment of the disposal by the distributing company, under the chargeable gains legislation, remains unchanged.

Amendments to worldwide debt cap

A number of measures are proposed to improve the operation of the worldwide debt cap. These will have effect for periods of account ending on or after the date of Royal Assent to Finance Bill 2012.

The new rules will include an ability to opt out of the *de minimis* limits of the net financing deduction and income amounts, and rules to deal with mergers, acquisitions and demergers of groups, dormant companies and elections for companies to be treated as authorised companies and treasury companies. There will also be an anti-avoidance provision and a power to make regulations dealing with proposed changes in accounting standards.

Changes to UK GAAP

Significant changes to UK GAAP are anticipated during 2012. In a number of areas these are likely to result in accounting adjustments on transition from old to new UK GAAP and the relevant tax legislation will be amended to ensure that on a change of accounting policy, income is taxed once and only once and expenditure is allowed once and only once.

The measure will apply to changes in accounting policy of businesses where accounts are prepared after 1 January 2012, even if the accounts are for accounting periods starting before that date.

Oil and gas

Supplementary charge

New rules will ensure that the supplementary charge applies to ring fence chargeable gains and to confirm that the scope of the supplementary charge matches the scope of the ring fenced corporation tax. These measures are effective from 6 December 2011.

Field allowances

The field allowance reduces the amount of adjusted ring fence profits for the accounting period on which the supplementary charge is imposed. The Government wants to 'encourage investment and innovation' by the oil and gas industries (particularly gas, according to the Chancellor's Budget Speech, as it is lower in carbon).

Changes to the field allowance legislation will be made by secondary legislation to:

- Increase the amount of small field allowance and to increase the size of the field qualifying for the maximum allowance.
- Introduce a new £3 billion field allowance for new fields that meet the certain qualification criteria, expected to apply to the West of Shetland.

The extension of the field allowance will have effect at a future date to be decided by Government.

The changes to the small field allowance and West of Shetland allowance will apply to fields with development authorisation on or after 21 March 2012.

Stamp taxes

Stamp duty land tax: rate in respect of residential property where consideration over £2 million

There is an increase in the rate of stamp duty land tax for residential property over £2 million from 5% to 7% from 22 March 2012. This will impact on freehold purchases and the grants or assignments of leases, where the consideration (or premium for the grant of a lease) is over £2 million. It may also impact on exchanges of land, transfers to connected companies and partnerships where the property value is in excess of £2 million.

The legislation will include transitional provisions which mean that if exchange took place before 22 March 2012, the old rates will continue to apply.

Stamp duty land tax: enveloping of high value residential properties

This is a measure to combat the perceived large scale avoidance of stamp duty by owning property though companies (typically offshore companies). When the measure applies stamp duty land tax will be charged on the acquisition at 15%.

The charge will take effect when the purchaser is a 'non-natural' person, which would include a company, a collective investment scheme and a partnership in which a non-natural person is a partner.

Of particular note is that there will be exclusions from charge for property developers and corporate trustees – in certain circumstances.

This measure will apply from 21 March 2012, although there are transitional provisions for purchases where exchange occurred before that date.

Stamp duty land tax avoidance

See *Anti-avoidance*.

Stamp duty land tax and stamp duty: relief for NHS bodies

This relief is not of general application since it only applies to acquisitions of interests in UK land by certain NHS bodies.

The measure will update stamp duty land tax (SDLT) relief for acquisitions by NHS bodies to take into account changes under the Health and Social Care Bill. From its introduction, the relief will be available for acquisitions by the NHS Commissioning Board and clinical commissioning groups provided for by the Health and Social Care Bill, NHS foundation trusts, NHS trusts and Local Health Boards in Wales, and Health and Social Services trusts in Northern Ireland. Until their abolition, relief will also be available for acquisitions by NHS trusts in England and by Primary Care Trusts. An equivalent, obsolete stamp duty relief is removed.

The measure will have effect from Royal Assent to Finance Bill 2012.

Stamp duty land tax: disclosure of tax avoidance schemes

See *Anti-avoidance*.

Indirect tax, customs duties, etc

Value added tax (VAT)

VAT registration threshold

The VAT registration and deregistration thresholds will be changed so that:

- the taxable turnover threshold, which determines whether a person must be registered for VAT, will be increased from £73,000 to £77,000;
- the taxable turnover threshold, which determines whether a person may apply for deregistration, will be increased from £71,000 to £75,000; and
- the registration and deregistration threshold for relevant acquisitions from other EU Member States will also be increased from £73,000 to £77,000.

A statutory instrument laid on 21 March 2011 will apply the revised thresholds with effect from 1 April 2012.

Fuel scale charges

Fuel Scale Charges will change with effect from 1 May 2012. The revised rates are included in the 'Overview of Tax Legislation and Rates' document published on Budget Day, which can be accessed from the HMRC website (http://www.hmrc.gov.uk/budget2012/ootlar.htm).

Low value consignment relief

The low value consignment relief (LVCR) allows imports with a value of less than £15 to be imported VAT free. This concession has been exploited by many high street retailers who have set up off-shore operations in the Channel Islands selling mail order CDs, DVDs etc VAT free into the UK.

As a result of pressure from business associations the Government has announced that from 1 April 2012 LVCR will no longer apply to goods sent to the UK from the Channel Islands.

The change to LVCR will not affect the existing import reliefs for gifts from outside the EU, including from the Channel Islands. This relief applies to non-commercial consignments, such as gifts sent to family members or friends.

Cost sharing exemption

Following consultation over summer 2011, legislation will be introduced to bring the EU VAT Cost Sharing Exemption into UK law. This proposal will affect all businesses and organisations that have exempt and/or non-business activities for VAT purposes and that want to join with similar businesses and organisations to share costs. Eligible businesses and organisations include charities, universities, further education colleges, banks, housing associations, and insurance companies.

This measure allows groups to exempt from VAT, supplies made to their members, provided certain conditions are satisfied.

The measure will have effect on and after the date of Royal Assent to Finance Bill 2012. The legislation will introduce a new Group 16 to Schedule 9 to the VAT Act 1994 – Supplies of services by groups involving cost sharing.

Tackling VAT fraud on imported road vehicles

From 2013, a person bringing a new or used road vehicle into the UK for permanent use on UK roads will have to notify HMRC within 14 days of the arrival of the vehicle in the UK and before registering it with the DVLA. In the case of an acquisition of a new road vehicle from within the EU, private individuals and non-VAT registered businesses will be required to pay any VAT due at the time of notification. VAT registered customers will continue to make payment via their VAT return.

Until HMRC is notified and any VAT due has been paid, or for VAT registered businesses is assessed as 'secure', it will not be possible to licence and register a vehicle with the DVLA.

Some arrivals into the UK will be specifically excluded from the requirement to notify i.e. visitors bringing their vehicles into the UK temporarily, UK residents returning from a holiday with their road vehicle, private importers, and vehicles brought into the UK under secure schemes approved by the DVLA.

Online registration and tranche two of online filing of returns

An enhanced online system for VAT registration, de-registration, and changes to business details will be introduced from October 2012. Also from that date, twenty VAT forms will no longer be required by legislation.

Of great importance to overseas businesses the VAT threshold for businesses not established in the UK will be removed from

Summary of Budget Proposals 21 March 2012

1 December 2012 and they will not benefit from the UK VAT registration thresholds. Therefore any overseas business (including other EU businesses) trading in the UK (where the place of supply is the UK) will be required to register for VAT.

For VAT periods beginning on or after 1 April 2012, the second tranche of existing VAT businesses (with a VAT exclusive turnover of under £100,000), will be mandated to file VAT returns online and make electronic payments.

VAT grouping – extra statutory concession 3.2.2

Legislation will be introduced to bring into law a long standing concession on the valuation of certain reverse charges applicable to VAT groups. This will allow the reverse charge (which obliges the recipient of a supply to account for VAT on that supply as output tax) to be based on the cost of services purchased by the group members established overseas.

Treatment of public bodies

Legislation will be introduced to amend UK law to ensure that there is clear transposition of EU agreements relating to the VAT treatment of public bodies carrying out their statutory duties. Since the measure simply involves the technical implementation of EU law, which is already implemented in practice, there has not been a consultation period.

In practice public bodies should see no change to their existing tax treatment as a result of the legislative changes.

Proposals and consultation for removing anomalies in the VAT system

Hot takeaway food and premises

There is a change clarifying the definition of 'hot takeaway food' to confirm that all food, including drinks (with the exception of freshly baked bread) that is above ambient air temperature when provided to the customer is standard-rated. It also clarifies the definition of 'premises' to confirm that: (i) all food sold for consumption on the premises on which it is supplied; and (ii) all food sold for consumption in areas adjacent to those premises or in areas shared with other retailers, is subject to VAT at the standard rate.

Examples of products affected by the change include: rotisserie chicken products, pies, pasties, toasted sandwiches etc, when *above* the ambient air temperature at the time they are provided to the customer.

Sports nutrition drinks

This measure will tax sports nutrition drinks at the standard rate, ensuring that all sports drinks receive the same treatment whether or not they are consumed for nutritional purposes.

Self-storage

There is a measure to tax all provision of self-storage. Self-storage businesses provide their customers with a clearly defined lockable space to which the customer has access for the purpose of storing goods. The measure provides consistency of treatment within the self- storage industry; levels the playing field between providers of self-storage and providers of other storage; and addresses tax avoidance.

Hairdresser's chair rental

This measure will make it clear in legislation that the supply of facilities to a hairdresser is taxable at the standard rate and is not an exempt licence to occupy land.

Holiday caravans

There is a measure to tax the sale of holiday caravans (mainly static holiday caravans), ensuring that the sale of all holiday caravans is standard-rated, while preserving the zero-rate for residential caravans. The current size restrictions for zero-rating will therefore be removed and a new test will restrict the zero-rate to the sale of caravans that conform to British Standard BS3632 (or equivalent), which indicates that the caravan is designed and manufactured for continuous all year round occupation, and is therefore suitable for residential accommodation.

Approved alterations to listed buildings

This measure will remove the zero-rate for alterations to protected buildings, mostly listed residential dwellings but also listed buildings used for charitable and other residential purposes. It does not apply to supplies of repairs and maintenance which are already taxable.

The change removes zero-rating from building materials and construction services supplied in the course of an approved alteration to a listed building.

The zero-rate for the first sale or long lease of a substantially reconstructed protected building will be restricted so that the current-zero rating for reconstructions where 60% of the reconstruction costs are approved alterations is removed but zero–rating is retained for buildings reconstructed from a shell.

Some owners of listed buildings and developers will already have entered into binding contracts for approved alteration works and associated construction materials prior to Budget Day. The following transitional arrangements will be put in place to allow sufficient time for contracted works to be completed and for developers to sell or make a long lease of substantially reconstructed protected buildings, while continuing to qualify for the zero-rate.

Approved alterations and the sale of a substantially reconstructed building will continue to benefit from the zero-rate if performed up to 20 March 2013 (i.e. one year after Budget day). Any works performed after that date will be standard-rated.

Excise duty

Tobacco products duty

The Chancellor announced 5% increase in duty on tobacco products across the board. This will add, for example, 37 pence to the price of 20 cigarettes and 20 pence to a 25g packet of pipe tobacco. This will take effect from 6pm on the date of the Budget (21 March 2012).

Machine games duty

The Finance Bill 2012 will include a measure to introduce reform of the method of taxation for gaming machines: cash jackpot slot machines and the like. Currently, the taxation is by annual licence, payable in bands according to the stake and prize and is called amusement machine licence duty (AMLD). This will change to machine games duty (MGD), a system whereby operators of the machines are taxed on their net takings, bringing the taxation into line with other gaming taxes. The machines operators will be taxed in two bands according to the maximum prize and size of the stake to play the machine. VAT legislation will also be amended to exclude money staked on such machines from supply VAT. The intended start date of this measure is 1 February 2013.

Transitional measures affecting AMLD will be announced at a later date and will include an interim increase in AMLD in line with the RPI.

Gambling duties

In a measure aimed at encouraging remote gaming companies (internet-based casinos etc) to remain based in the UK, the Finance Bill will introduce measures to avoid double taxation on such concerns where overseas tax administrations impose 'place of consumption' based taxation on such companies. The measures will come into effect in April 2012.

Gaming duty will increase in line with RPI.

Alcohol duties

A duty increase of 2% across the board on alcohol products will be introduced with effect from 26 March 2012. This will add 3 pence to the price of a pint of beer, and 11 pence to a bottle of wine.

Measures intended to remove redundant legislation in the Alcoholic Liquor Duties Act 1979, s 22 will be introduced. Rectifiers and compounders of alcoholic spirit to be exported from the UK often claim back UK excise duty through this legislation. It is also possible to do so by means of the Excise Goods Drawback Regulations 1995. Thus the redundant legislation will be repealed with effect from the date of Royal Assent to Finance Bill 2012.

Also, an historic exemption from excise duty for 'black beer', a strong malt beer with a high original gravity, is to be removed bringing the product into line with the taxation on other beers. This will come into effect in April 2013.

Air passenger duty

Air passenger duty (APD), currently applied per passenger journey on commercial airlines, is to be extended to smaller aircraft and, in particular, flights made on luxury business jets, which will carry duty at twice the current levels of APD for business and first class flights. The change is expected to be made by reducing the *de minimis* weight limit on aircraft subject to APD from 10 tonnes to 5.7 tonnes. The exemption applied to emergency flights will remain in force.

Also, Finance Bill 2012 will devolve responsibility for setting APD rates on long haul flights commencing from airports in Northern Ireland to the Northern Ireland Assembly. The measure is intended to help preserve and boost vital services to North America from Northern Ireland airports.

Vehicle excise duty

Vehicle excise duty will increase in line with RPI for all vehicles except heavy goods vehicles (HGVs). The HGV rates will be frozen for the tax year 2012/13.

Climate change levy (CCL)

Carbon price support rates

Legislation will be introduced in Finance Bill 2012 to:
- ensure that supplies of fossil fuels (e.g. coal and gas) to combined heat and power (CHP) stations and power generators fitted with carbon capture and storage technology can benefit from lower carbon price support (CPS) rates of CCL;
- require large-scale electricity generators to self-account for these CPS rates, and change the basis of taxation for fuels such as coal from weight (i.e. per kilogram) to heat (i.e. per kilojoule); and

- set the CPS rates of CCL for 2014/15.

The reliefs outlined above also require secondary legislation, which will also set out the detailed administrative provisions to enable HMRC to administer the CPS rates of CCL. Other secondary legislation will also provide that oils used in electricity generation will no longer be fully relieved of fuel duty, which will, in effect, make such oils subject to CPS rates of fuel duty, with an effective lower rate applying to oils used in CHP stations. All these changes take effect from 1 April 2013.

Change to the reduced rate on electricity

Legislation will be introduced to amend the reduced rate of CCL on electricity only from 35% to 10% from 1 April 2013. This amendment will help mitigate the impacts on energy-intensive industry of the carbon price floor from the same date. The legislation will also correct an omission in the legislation introduced in Finance Act 2010, which amended the reduced rate of CCL from 20% to 35% for all taxable commodities.

Rates

The Finance Bill 2012 will amend the CCL rates from 1 April 2013.

Budget 2012 announced the CPS rate for 2014/15. It also announced a number of changes to the CPS rate for solid fuels following consultation:
- coal with a calorific value of more than 15 gigajoules per tonne will be the only taxable solid fuel;
- coal will be taxed on its calorific value (i.e. joule), rather than its weight (i.e. kilogram);
- the rate for coal will reflect the average calorific value of coal used to generate electricity within the UK; and
- the rate for solid fuel for 2013/14 that was announced at Budget 2011 will be amended.

A number of other changes to the carbon price floor were also announced following consultation, including:
- supplies of fossil fuels to combined heat and power (CHP) stations registered under the CHP Quality Assurance pro-

gramme will be exempt from the CPS rates if they are intended to be used to generate heat;

- all generators liable to pay the CPS rates of climate change levy (CCL) will be required to register with HMRC if they are not already registered for CCL, and account for the CPS rates of CCL due;
- generators, and any connected persons, that have a combined generation capacity of 2 megawatts or lower will not be liable to the CPS rates of CCL; and
- supplies of fossil fuels to generating stations fitted with carbon capture and storage technology will be entitled to a proportionate abated CPS rate of CCL to reflect the percentage of carbon dioxide abated.

Reform of climate change agreements

The climate change agreement scheme will be extended to 2023 and the current participating sectors will continue to be eligible. Following consultation in September and October 2011, legislation will be introduced to simplify and streamline the scheme from 1 April 2013.

Removal of the exemption for indirect supplies of combined heat and power electricity

Legislation will be introduced to withdraw the exemption from CCL for supplies of electricity generated in a CHP station that are made by an electricity utility to business energy consumers. Electricity utility companies will be able to continue to allocate CHP levy exemption certificates relating to generation made before 1 April 2013 until 31 March 2018.

Metal recycling processes

Legislation will be introduced in Finance Bill 2012 to introduce a lower rate of 20% of the full rates of CCL for supplies of taxable commodities used in the recycling of steel and aluminium, from 1 April 2012.

Anti-avoidance

Capital allowances: anti-avoidance

There are anti-avoidance rules that deny first-year allowances or annual investment allowances for expenditure on plant and machinery, and restrict the amount on which the buyer of plant and machinery can claim capital allowances, which apply to transactions between connected persons, sale and leaseback transactions and transactions to obtain allowances.

The definition of this last category is being broadened so that the legislation will now apply to transactions which have a tax avoidance purpose or are part of, or occur as a result of, a scheme or arrangement with a tax avoidance purpose. The wider rule will apply if the main purpose, or one of the main purposes, of a party is to enable a person to obtain a greater capital allowance in respect of the plant and machinery than that intended.

The counteraction to such tax avoidance will also be broadened to allow the tax advantage to be cancelled out, either by restricting the expenditure on which the buyer can claim capital allowances or by reversing a timing advantage. These new counteractions are in addition to the denial of first-year allowances or annual investment allowances.

The anti-avoidance rules for transactions between connected persons and sales and leasebacks are not changed.

The new rules will have effect in relation to expenditure incurred on or after 1 April 2012 for corporation tax purposes or 6 April 2012 for income tax purposes.

There are also changes to the anti-avoidance rules relating to the acquisition of plant and machinery from a manufacturer or supplier, to counter a marketed tax avoidance scheme. However, this will only apply where the transaction has an avoidance purpose and not to connected persons or sale and leaseback transactions. (The original announcement, in December 2011, was that the change would apply to connected persons or sale and leaseback transactions between 12 August 2011 – when the change was first announced – until April 2012.)

Summary of Budget Proposals 21 March 2012

Inheritance tax (IHT): avoidance using offshore trusts

This provision is included in response to avoidance schemes exploiting the IHT 'excluded property' rules. Through the use of a series of transactions the schemes enable a UK domiciled individual to acquire an interest in an offshore trust thus converting assets which should be taxable into excluded property and reducing the value of the estate subject to IHT. The measure ensures that any reduction in the value of a person's estate as a result of the arrangements is chargeable to IHT.

Stamp duty land tax avoidance

There is a very targeted anti-avoidance measure designed to prevent the stamp duty land tax sub-sale rules from applying where the second step of the sub-sale is the grant or assignment of an option.

The provision will take effect from 21 March 2012.

Stamp duty land tax: disclosure of tax avoidance schemes

This is a measure targeted at users and promoters of stamp duty land tax (SDLT) avoidance schemes. Under the disclosure of tax avoidance schemes (DOTAS) rules certain SDLT tax avoidance schemes do not need to be disclosed. Among these are schemes which were in use prior to the extension of the DOTAS rules to SDLT and schemes targeted at residential properties under £1 million or commercial properties under £5 million. As a result of this schemes have arisen (or rather been continued) with the aim of avoiding the need to make disclosure.

Following Royal Assent to Finance Bill 2012, regulations will remove the grandfathering rules as they relate to schemes involving transfers of rights under FA 2003, s 45 and the financial limits for disclosure.

Tax avoidance: corporate settlor-interested trusts

Income which arises under a settlement is treated for income tax purposes as income of the settlor if the income arises from property in which the settlor has an interest; the tax charge being at the taxpayer's highest tax rate. Tax avoidance schemes have set up corporate settlor 'interest in possession' trusts with dividends being paid by a subsidiary of that company to avoid income tax that would otherwise be charged at higher or additional rates. This section amends the rules taxing the income as if it was the settlor's personal income.

Sale of lessor companies

The rules for the sale of plant and machinery lessor companies prevent a loss of tax when a lessor company is sold by bringing into charge an amount equivalent to any deferred tax profits of the lessor company when the company changes hands. However, tax avoidance schemes exploiting weaknesses in the legislation have been disclosed to HMRC, so changes will be made in the Finance Bill to bring the deferred tax profits of a lessor company into charge immediately before a lessor company comes within the charge to tonnage tax.

Further changes will prevent the losses of an accounting period following a change of ownership from being carried back against profits specifically brought into charge as a consequence of the sale of lessor company legislation.

The new rules will be effective from Budget Day, 21 March 2012.

Plant and machinery leasing: anti-avoidance

A lessee of plant or machinery under a long funding lease can claim capital allowances and must bring a disposal value into account at the end of the lease.

HMRC has seen arrangements in which 'payments connected to the lease for the benefit of the lessee have not been brought into account'. The new rules, effective for disposal events under long funding leases on or after 21 March 2012, will ensure that all payments connected with a long funding lease, or made as part of arrangements connected with the lease, are brought into account as intended, regardless of when they are paid. There will also be provision for the imposition of an arm's-length amount where the transaction is not carried out on arm's-length terms.

Life insurance policies: income tax avoidance

Gains made on life assurance policies are taxed under the 'chargeable event' regime whereby the amount of a gain chargeable to income tax is calculated as being the difference between the value of benefits paid *from* a policy and the total of premiums paid *into* the policy plus gains arising earlier in the life of a policy. Currently those earlier gains are deductible whether they had been subject to tax or not (for example, if the taxpayer had been non-domiciled). This provision rules that to be included in the gain calculation the earlier gain must have been subject to tax.

Site restoration payments

Capital expenditure on site restoration payments is a deductible expense in the computation of taxable profits. Under this provision deduction will not be allowed on any payment arising from arrangements to which a person is party the main purpose, or one of the main purposes of the arrangements being the obtaining of a tax deduction.

HMRC administration

Tax agreement between the United Kingdom and Switzerland

This measure will give effect to an agreement dated 6 October 2011 and the protocol dated 20 March 2012 between the governments of the UK and Switzerland. The agreement has four main effects:

- It provides for a one-off levy to be applied to accounts in Switzerland held directly or indirectly by individuals who are resident in the UK unless the individual authorises disclosure of those accounts. Compliant individuals should authorise disclosure and so avoid the levy.
- It applies a withholding tax to income and gains arising on those Swiss accounts from 1 January 2013. Compliant individuals may authorise disclosure and avoid the withholding tax.

- There will be a levy on the assets of an individual who dies after 1 January 2013 with Swiss assets (unless disclosure is made) to satisfy liability to UK inheritance tax.
- It provides for enhanced exchange of information between the tax authorities of the two countries.

This measure is expected to yield between £4 billion and £7 billion in additional revenues.

Information powers

There will be a new power allowing HMRC to require a data-holder to provide a person's name, address and date of birth from identifying information held by HMRC and provided to the data-holder. This will enable HMRC to obtain information from the data-holder, following which HMRC will be able to use their existing information powers.

The new power will not require tribunal approval, but in line with the existing rules, the power may only be exercised by an authorised officer of HMRC and the data-holder will have the same right of appeal against a notice.

The new power will be effective from the date of Royal Assent to Finance Bill 2012.

Tax agents: dishonest conduct

Legislation will be introduced in Finance Bill 2012 to allow HMRC to issue a tax agent with a conduct notice if it has been determined that they have engaged in dishonest conduct. This notice would be subject to appeal.

Subject to prior approval by the First-tier Tribunal, HMRC would be able to issue a File Access Notice requiring production of the working papers of tax agents found to have engaged in dishonest conduct. Where working papers are no longer in the power or possession of the tax agent, HMRC would be able to request these from a third party.

There will be a civil penalty for dishonest conduct in an amount of up to £50,000. In cases where full disclosure was not made, HMRC would be able to publish details of the penalised tax agent.

Summary of Budget Proposals 21 March 2012

Incapacitated persons: a modern approach

This measure is intended to ensure that by removing the current definition of 'incapacitated person' from the Taxes Management Act 1970 those people who are incapacitated will have the same rights and powers as if they were not incapacitated.

Those rights and obligations will though be able to be exercised and met by the person's representative acting in a representative capacity (i.e. making decisions, signing documents etc on their behalf).

This measure will take effect on or after the date on which Finance Bill 2012 receives Royal Assent for SDLT, and from the 2012/13 tax year for other taxes.

Office of Tax Simplification (OTS)

OTS: review of reliefs

The OTS was created in July 2010 with the remit to provide the Government with independent advice on simplifying the UK tax system and in particular identifying tax reliefs to be abolished or simplified. The following will be abolished as from 1 April 2013 for companies and 6 April 2013 for unincorporated businesses and individuals (unless another date is specified).

Mineral royalties

Mineral royalties relief allowed businesses to treat 50% of the total amount of eligible mineral royalties received as a chargeable gain and the remaining 50% subject to the then higher rates of income or corporation tax. Relief is no longer necessary as tax rates are now much lower than when the relief was enacted.

Stamp duty land tax: disadvantaged areas relief

SDLT is not levied for purchases of residential property priced less than £150,000 in areas designated as 'disadvantaged'. The relief is abolished as there is no evidence that the relief encourages ownership in disadvantaged areas.

Grants for giving up agricultural land

Grants given to individuals for not working areas of agricultural land were exempt from capital gains tax. Relief is no longer necessary as no such grants have been made for a number of years.

Angostura bitters and black beer

The exemption of these drinks from Customs and Excise duty has been repealed as from 1 April 2013.

Luncheon vouchers

The Government believes that the value of the 15 pence allowance per working day has been eroded by inflation and that the original objective is no longer relevant.

Certain payments arising from a reduction in pool betting duty

This is no longer relevant as the payments ceased in March 2004.

Stamp duty: certain transactions in shares

Relief no longer applies for transfers of shares in connection with nationalisation and certain other company share transfers.

Tax reserve certificates

These certificates have not been issued since 1975, when they were replaced by certificates of tax deposit. A small amount of interest will have accrued payable on redemption and exemption from tax for interest payable will remain for certificates redeemed before April 2013.

Payments for the benefit of family members

Maximum tax relief of £20 could be claimed by employees who were required by their employer to make payments to secure a provision for their surviving spouse/civil partner or children.

Relief is no longer necessary as the pensions code provides relief for similar expenditure.

Capital allowances

- Safety at sports grounds – works have been completed.
- Flat conversion allowances – insufficient uptake.

Stamp duty – transactions in land

This is no longer relevant as it was replaced by stamp duty land tax in 2003.

Harbour reorganisation schemes: corporation tax and stamp duty

There is no evidence of recent or planned use.

Pensions for 1947 redundancies

Provided for the payment of specific pensions – no longer relevant.

Deeply discounted securities: incidental expenses

Relief will be removed as from 6 April 2015.

Life assurance premium relief

Tax relief of 12.5% on the premium paid on policies issued before 14 March 1984 is abolished for premiums due on or after 6 April 2015 for both individuals and employers who pay under an employer-financed retirement benefit scheme (EFRBS). This is to comply with the new regulations required for the taxation of life assurance companies.

Class 4 NICs – deduction for certain losses

This relief was a transitional provision relevant for the introduction of independent taxation of spouses in 1990; it is no longer relevant.

NICs exemption for certain apprentices and students coming to the UK

This provides exemption from Class 1 National Insurance contributions for the first 52 weeks where an individual who is not ordinarily resident in the UK meets certain criteria. The exemption has limited use as it does not apply to individuals from within the European Economic Area or from countries with which the UK has a Reciprocal Agreement or Double Contribution Convention.

Class 1A NICs – exemption for prescribed general earnings

This is no longer relevant as the exemption applied on certain specified expenses incurred before April 1998.

Certain payments to mariners

The specific payments referred to are no longer made.

Cycle to work days – provision of meals

There is insufficient uptake; the value of the relief is low compared with the cost of implementation.

National Insurance Contributions – From 6 April 2012

CLASS 1: EMPLOYED PERSONS (NOT CONTRACTED OUT)

Rate for **Employees**

(a) Men under 65, women under 60

Earnings up to 146 p.w.	Nil
Earnings between £146 and £817 p.w.	12.0%
Earnings over £817 p.w.	2.0%

(b) Men over 65, women over 60	Nil

(c) Married women and widows liable at reduced rate

Earnings up to £146 p.w.	Nil
Earnings between £146 p.w. and £817 p.w	5.85%
Earnings over £817 p.w.	2.0%

Rate for **Employers**

All categories (a)–(c) above

Earnings up to £144 p.w.	Nil
Earnings over £144 p.w.	13.8%

CLASS 1: EMPLOYED PERSONS (CONTRACTED OUT)

Rate for **Employees**

(a) Men under 65, women under 60

Earnings up to £146 p.w.	Nil
Earnings between £146 and £817 p.w.	10.6%
Earnings over £817 p.w.	2.0%
Rebate on earnings from £107 and £146 p.w.	1.4%

(b) Men over 65, women over 60	Nil

(c) Married women and widows liable at reduced rate

Earnings up to £146 p.w.	Nil
Earnings between £146 p.w. and £817 p.w	5.85%
Earnings over £817 p.w.	2.0%

Rate for **Employers** operating a	Salary related scheme	Money purchase scheme
(a) Men under 65, women under 60		
Earnings up to £144 p.w.	Nil	Nil
Earnings between £144 and £817 p.w.	10.4%	13.8%
Earnings over £817 p.w.	13.8%	13.8%
Rebate on earnings from £102 and £136 p.w.	3.4%	Abolished from 6 April 2012
(b) Men over 65, women over 60	Not allowed to contract out	
(c) Married women and widows liable at reduced rate	As (a) above	

CLASS 2: SELF-EMPLOYED PERSONS

Men under 65, women under 60 (Exemption claimable if anticipated earnings less than £5,595)	£2.65 p.w.

CLASS 3: VOLUNTARY CONTRIBUTIONS

Men and women (but only for years before the person reaches the age of 65 or 60 respectively)	£13.25 p.w.

CLASS 4: SELF-EMPLOYED PERSONS

Rate payable (by men under 65 and women under 60)

on profits between £7,605 and £42,475 per year	9.0%
over £42,475 per year	2.0%

(a) Payable on dividends otherwise taxable at the additional rate
(b) Dividend trust rate

2012/13   Dividend Additional Rate (a)   42·5%
Dividend Trust Rate (b)

£ or p	Tax £ or p	£ or p	Tax £ or p	£	Tax £	£	Tax £	£	Tax £	£	Tax £	£	Tax £	£	Tax £	£	Tax £	£	Tax £
1	0.43	51	21.68	101	42.93	151	64.18	201	85.43	251	106.68	301	127.93	351	149.18	401	170.43	451	191.68
2	0.85	52	22.10	102	43.35	152	64.60	202	85.85	252	107.10	302	128.35	352	149.60	402	170.85	452	192.10
3	1.28	53	22.53	103	43.78	153	65.03	203	86.28	253	107.53	303	128.78	353	150.03	403	171.28	453	192.53
4	1.70	54	22.95	104	44.20	154	65.45	204	86.70	254	107.95	304	129.20	354	150.45	404	171.70	454	192.95
5	2.13	55	23.38	105	44.63	155	65.88	205	87.13	255	108.38	305	129.63	355	150.88	405	172.13	455	193.38
6	2.55	56	23.80	106	45.05	156	66.30	206	87.55	256	108.80	306	130.05	356	151.30	406	172.55	456	193.80
7	2.98	57	24.23	107	45.48	157	66.73	207	87.98	257	109.23	307	130.48	357	151.73	407	172.98	457	194.23
8	3.40	58	24.65	108	45.90	158	67.15	208	88.40	258	109.65	308	130.90	358	152.15	408	173.40	458	194.65
9	3.83	59	25.08	109	46.33	159	67.58	209	88.83	259	110.08	309	131.33	359	152.58	409	173.83	459	195.08
10	4.25	60	25.50	110	46.75	160	68.00	210	89.25	260	110.50	310	131.75	360	153.00	410	174.25	460	195.50
11	4.68	61	25.93	111	47.18	161	68.43	211	89.68	261	110.93	311	132.18	361	153.43	411	174.68	461	195.93
12	5.10	62	26.35	112	47.60	162	68.85	212	90.10	262	111.35	312	132.60	362	153.85	412	175.10	462	196.35
13	5.53	63	26.78	113	48.03	163	69.28	213	90.53	263	111.78	313	133.03	363	154.28	413	175.53	463	196.78
14	5.95	64	27.20	114	48.45	164	69.70	214	90.95	264	112.20	314	133.45	364	154.70	414	175.95	464	197.20
15	6.38	65	27.63	115	48.88	165	70.13	215	91.38	265	112.63	315	133.88	365	155.13	415	176.38	465	197.63
16	6.80	66	28.05	116	49.30	166	70.55	216	91.80	266	113.05	316	134.30	366	155.55	416	176.80	466	198.05
17	7.23	67	28.48	117	49.73	167	70.98	217	92.23	267	113.48	317	134.73	367	155.98	417	177.23	467	198.48
18	7.65	68	28.90	118	50.15	168	71.40	218	92.65	268	113.90	318	135.15	368	156.40	418	177.65	468	198.90
19	8.08	69	29.33	119	50.58	169	71.83	219	93.08	269	114.33	319	135.58	369	156.83	419	178.08	469	199.33
20	8.50	70	29.75	120	51.00	170	72.25	220	93.50	270	114.75	320	136.00	370	157.25	420	178.50	470	199.75
21	8.93	71	30.18	121	51.43	171	72.68	221	93.93	271	115.18	321	136.43	371	157.68	421	178.93	471	200.18
22	9.35	72	30.60	122	51.85	172	73.10	222	94.35	272	115.60	322	136.85	372	158.10	422	179.35	472	200.60
23	9.78	73	31.03	123	52.28	173	73.53	223	94.78	273	116.03	323	137.28	373	158.53	423	179.78	473	201.03
24	10.20	74	31.45	124	52.70	174	73.95	224	95.20	274	116.45	324	137.70	374	158.95	424	180.20	474	201.45
25	10.63	75	31.88	125	53.13	175	74.38	225	95.63	275	116.88	325	138.13	375	159.38	425	180.63	475	201.88
26	11.05	76	32.30	126	53.55	176	74.80	226	96.05	276	117.30	326	138.55	376	159.80	426	181.05	476	202.30
27	11.48	77	32.73	127	53.98	177	75.23	227	96.48	277	117.73	327	138.98	377	160.23	427	181.48	477	202.73
28	11.90	78	33.15	128	54.40	178	75.65	228	96.90	278	118.15	328	139.40	378	160.65	428	181.90	478	203.15
29	12.33	79	33.58	129	54.83	179	76.08	229	97.33	279	118.58	329	139.83	379	161.08	429	182.33	479	203.58
30	12.75	80	34.00	130	55.25	180	76.50	230	97.75	280	119.00	330	140.25	380	161.50	430	182.75	480	204.00
31	13.18	81	34.43	131	55.68	181	76.93	231	98.18	281	119.43	331	140.68	381	161.93	431	183.18	481	204.43
32	13.60	82	34.85	132	56.10	182	77.35	232	98.60	282	119.85	332	141.10	382	162.35	432	183.60	482	204.85
33	14.03	83	35.28	133	56.53	183	77.78	233	99.03	283	120.28	333	141.53	383	162.78	433	184.03	483	205.28
34	14.45	84	35.70	134	56.95	184	78.20	234	99.45	284	120.70	334	141.95	384	163.20	434	184.45	484	205.70
35	14.88	85	36.13	135	57.38	185	78.63	235	99.88	285	121.13	335	142.38	385	163.63	435	184.88	485	206.13
36	15.30	86	36.55	136	57.80	186	79.05	236	100.30	286	121.55	336	142.80	386	164.05	436	185.30	486	206.55
37	15.73	87	36.98	137	58.23	187	79.48	237	100.73	287	121.98	337	143.23	387	164.48	437	185.73	487	206.98
38	16.15	88	37.40	138	58.65	188	79.90	238	101.15	288	122.40	338	143.65	388	164.90	438	186.15	488	207.40
39	16.58	89	37.83	139	59.08	189	80.33	239	101.58	289	122.83	339	144.08	389	165.33	439	186.58	489	207.83
40	17.00	90	38.25	140	59.50	190	80.75	240	102.00	290	123.25	340	144.50	390	165.75	440	187.00	490	208.25
41	17.43	91	38.68	141	59.93	191	81.18	241	102.43	291	123.68	341	144.93	391	166.18	441	187.43	491	208.68
42	17.85	92	39.10	142	60.35	192	81.60	242	102.85	292	124.10	342	145.35	392	166.60	442	187.85	492	209.10
43	18.28	93	39.53	143	60.78	193	82.03	243	103.28	293	124.53	343	145.78	393	167.03	443	188.28	493	209.53
44	18.70	94	39.95	144	61.20	194	82.45	244	103.70	294	124.95	344	146.20	394	167.45	444	188.70	494	209.95
45	19.13	95	40.38	145	61.63	195	82.88	245	104.13	295	125.38	345	146.63	395	167.88	445	189.13	495	210.38
46	19.55	96	40.80	146	62.05	196	83.30	246	104.55	296	125.80	346	147.05	396	168.30	446	189.55	496	210.80
47	19.98	97	41.23	147	62.48	197	83.73	247	104.98	297	126.23	347	147.48	397	168.73	447	189.98	497	211.23
48	20.40	98	41.65	148	62.90	198	84.15	248	105.40	298	126.65	348	147.90	398	169.15	448	190.40	498	211.65
49	20.83	99	42.08	149	63.33	199	84.58	249	105.83	299	127.08	349	148.33	399	169.58	449	190.83	499	212.08
50	21.25	100	42.50	150	63.75	200	85.00	250	106.25	300	127.50	350	148.75	400	170.00	450	191.25	500	212.50
On Tax	£1,000 £425		£1,500 £638		£2,000 £850		£2,500 £1,063		£3,000 £1,275		£3,500 £1,488		£4,000 £1,700		£4,500 £1,913		£5,000 £2,125	

50%   2012/13: Income Tax (a) Trusts (b)

(a) Additional rate payable on taxable income over £150,000.
(b) Trust rate (formerly known as 'the rate applicable to trusts').

£ or p	Tax £ or p	£ or p	Tax £ or p	£	Tax £	£	Tax £	£	Tax £	£	Tax £	£	Tax £	£	Tax £	£	Tax £	£	Tax £
1	0.50	51	25.50	101	50.50	151	75.50	201	100.50	251	125.50	301	150.50	351	175.50	401	200.50	451	225.50
2	1.00	52	26.00	102	51.00	152	76.00	202	101.00	252	126.00	302	151.00	352	176.00	402	201.00	452	226.00
3	1.50	53	26.50	103	51.50	153	76.50	203	101.50	253	126.50	303	151.50	353	176.50	403	201.50	453	226.50
4	2.00	54	27.00	104	52.00	154	77.00	204	102.00	254	127.00	304	152.00	354	177.00	404	202.00	454	227.00
5	2.50	55	27.50	105	52.50	155	77.50	205	102.50	255	127.50	305	152.50	355	177.50	405	202.50	455	227.50
6	3.00	56	28.00	106	53.00	156	78.00	206	103.00	256	128.00	306	153.00	356	178.00	406	203.00	456	228.00
7	3.50	57	28.50	107	53.50	157	78.50	207	103.50	257	128.50	307	153.50	357	178.50	407	203.50	457	228.50
8	4.00	58	29.00	108	54.00	158	79.00	208	104.00	258	129.00	308	154.00	358	179.00	408	204.00	458	229.00
9	4.50	59	29.50	109	54.50	159	79.50	209	104.50	259	129.50	309	154.50	359	179.50	409	204.50	459	229.50
10	5.00	60	30.00	110	55.00	160	80.00	210	105.00	260	130.00	310	155.00	360	180.00	410	205.00	460	230.00
11	5.50	61	30.50	111	55.50	161	80.50	211	105.50	261	130.50	311	155.50	361	180.50	411	205.50	461	230.50
12	6.00	62	31.00	112	56.00	162	81.00	212	106.00	262	131.00	312	156.00	362	181.00	412	206.00	462	231.00
13	6.50	63	31.50	113	56.50	163	81.50	213	106.50	263	131.50	313	156.50	363	181.50	413	206.50	463	231.50
14	7.00	64	32.00	114	57.00	164	82.00	214	107.00	264	132.00	314	157.00	364	182.00	414	207.00	464	232.00
15	7.50	65	32.50	115	57.50	165	82.50	215	107.50	265	132.50	315	157.50	365	182.50	415	207.50	465	232.50
16	8.00	66	33.00	116	58.00	166	83.00	216	108.00	266	133.00	316	158.00	366	183.00	416	208.00	466	233.00
17	8.50	67	33.50	117	58.50	167	83.50	217	108.50	267	133.50	317	158.50	367	183.50	417	208.50	467	233.50
18	9.00	68	34.00	118	59.00	168	84.00	218	109.00	268	134.00	318	159.00	368	184.00	418	209.00	468	234.00
19	9.50	69	34.50	119	59.50	169	84.50	219	109.50	269	134.50	319	159.50	369	184.50	419	209.50	469	234.50
20	10.00	70	35.00	120	60.00	170	85.00	220	110.00	270	135.00	320	160.00	370	185.00	420	210.00	470	235.00
21	10.50	71	35.50	121	60.50	171	85.50	221	110.50	271	135.50	321	160.50	371	185.50	421	210.50	471	235.50
22	11.00	72	36.00	122	61.00	172	86.00	222	111.00	272	136.00	322	161.00	372	186.00	422	211.00	472	236.00
23	11.50	73	36.50	123	61.50	173	86.50	223	111.50	273	136.50	323	161.50	373	186.50	423	211.50	473	236.50
24	12.00	74	37.00	124	62.00	174	87.00	224	112.00	274	137.00	324	162.00	374	187.00	424	212.00	474	237.00
25	12.50	75	37.50	125	62.50	175	87.50	225	112.50	275	137.50	325	162.50	375	187.50	425	212.50	475	237.50
26	13.00	76	38.00	126	63.00	176	88.00	226	113.00	276	138.00	326	163.00	376	188.00	426	213.00	476	238.00
27	13.50	77	38.50	127	63.50	177	88.50	227	113.50	277	138.50	327	163.50	377	188.50	427	213.50	477	238.50
28	14.00	78	39.00	128	64.00	178	89.00	228	114.00	278	139.00	328	164.00	378	189.00	428	214.00	478	239.00
29	14.50	79	39.50	129	64.50	179	89.50	229	114.50	279	139.50	329	164.50	379	189.50	429	214.50	479	239.50
30	15.00	80	40.00	130	65.00	180	90.00	230	115.00	280	140.00	330	165.00	380	190.00	430	215.00	480	240.00
31	15.50	81	40.50	131	65.50	181	90.50	231	115.50	281	140.50	331	165.50	381	190.50	431	215.50	481	240.50
32	16.00	82	41.00	132	66.00	182	91.00	232	116.00	282	141.00	332	166.00	382	191.00	432	216.00	482	241.00
33	16.50	83	41.50	133	66.50	183	91.50	233	116.50	283	141.50	333	166.50	383	191.50	433	216.50	483	241.50
34	17.00	84	42.00	134	67.00	184	92.00	234	117.00	284	142.00	334	167.00	384	192.00	434	217.00	484	242.00
35	17.50	85	42.50	135	67.50	185	92.50	235	117.50	285	142.50	335	167.50	385	192.50	435	217.50	485	242.50
36	18.00	86	43.00	136	68.00	186	93.00	236	118.00	286	143.00	336	168.00	386	193.00	436	218.00	486	243.00
37	18.50	87	43.50	137	68.50	187	93.50	237	118.50	287	143.50	337	168.50	387	193.50	437	218.50	487	243.50
38	19.00	88	44.00	138	69.00	188	94.00	238	119.00	288	144.00	338	169.00	388	194.00	438	219.00	488	244.00
39	19.50	89	44.50	139	69.50	189	94.50	239	119.50	289	144.50	339	169.50	389	194.50	439	219.50	489	244.50
40	20.00	90	45.00	140	70.00	190	95.00	240	120.00	290	145.00	340	170.00	390	195.00	440	220.00	490	245.00
41	20.50	91	45.50	141	70.50	191	95.50	241	120.50	291	145.50	341	170.50	391	195.50	441	220.50	491	245.50
42	21.00	92	46.00	142	71.00	192	96.00	242	121.00	292	146.00	342	171.00	392	196.00	442	221.00	492	246.00
43	21.50	93	46.50	143	71.50	193	96.50	243	121.50	293	146.50	343	171.50	393	196.50	443	221.50	493	246.50
44	22.00	94	47.00	144	72.00	194	97.00	244	122.00	294	147.00	344	172.00	394	197.00	444	222.00	494	247.00
45	22.50	95	47.50	145	72.50	195	97.50	245	122.50	295	147.50	345	172.50	395	197.50	445	222.50	495	247.50
46	23.00	96	48.00	146	73.00	196	98.00	246	123.00	296	148.00	346	173.00	396	198.00	446	223.00	496	248.00
47	23.50	97	48.50	147	73.50	197	98.50	247	123.50	297	148.50	347	173.50	397	198.50	447	223.50	497	248.50
48	24.00	98	49.00	148	74.00	198	99.00	248	124.00	298	149.00	348	174.00	398	199.00	448	224.00	498	249.00
49	24.50	99	49.50	149	74.50	199	99.50	249	124.50	299	149.50	349	174.50	399	199.50	449	224.50	499	249.50
50	25.00	100	50.00	150	75.00	200	100.00	250	125.00	300	150.00	350	175.00	400	200.00	450	225.00	500	250.00

On	£1,000		£1,500		£2,000		£2,500		£3,000		£3,500		£4,000		£4,500		£5,000		
Tax	£500		£750		£1,000		£1,250		£1,500		£1,750		£2,000		£2,250		£2,500		

Dividend Tax Credits   10·0%

Net dividend £ or p	Tax credit £ or p	Net dividend £ or p	Tax credit £ or p	Net dividend £	Tax credit £	Net dividend £	Tax credit £	Net dividend £	Tax credit £	Net dividend £	Tax credit £	Net dividend £	Tax credit £	Net dividend £	Tax credit £	Net dividend £	Tax credit £	Net dividend £	Tax credit £
1	0·11	51	5·67	101	11·22	151	16·78	201	22·33	251	27·89	301	33·44	351	39·00	401	44·56	451	50·11
2	0·22	52	5·78	102	11·33	152	16·89	202	22·44	252	28·00	302	33·56	352	39·11	402	44·67	452	50·22
3	0·33	53	5·89	103	11·44	153	17·00	203	22·56	253	28·11	303	33·67	353	39·22	403	44·78	453	50·33
4	0·44	54	6·00	104	11·56	154	17·11	204	22·67	254	28·22	304	33·78	354	39·33	404	44·89	454	50·44
5	0·56	55	6·11	105	11·67	155	17·22	205	22·78	255	28·33	305	33·89	355	39·44	405	45·00	455	50·56
6	0·67	56	6·22	106	11·78	156	17·33	206	22·89	256	28·44	306	34·00	356	39·56	406	45·11	456	50·67
7	0·78	57	6·33	107	11·89	157	17·44	207	23·00	257	28·56	307	34·11	357	39·67	407	45·22	457	50·78
8	0·89	58	6·44	108	12·00	158	17·56	208	23·11	258	28·67	308	34·22	358	39·78	408	45·33	458	50·89
9	1·00	59	6·56	109	12·11	159	17·67	209	23·22	259	28·78	309	34·33	359	39·89	409	45·44	459	51·00
10	1·11	60	6·67	110	12·22	160	17·78	210	23·33	260	28·89	310	34·44	360	40·00	410	45·56	460	51·11
11	1·22	61	6·78	111	12·33	161	17·89	211	23·44	261	29·00	311	34·56	361	40·11	411	45·67	461	51·22
12	1·33	62	6·89	112	12·44	162	18·00	212	23·56	262	29·11	312	34·67	362	40·22	412	45·78	462	51·33
13	1·44	63	7·00	113	12·56	163	18·11	213	23·67	263	29·22	313	34·78	363	40·33	413	45·89	463	51·44
14	1·56	64	7·11	114	12·67	164	18·22	214	23·78	264	29·33	314	34·89	364	40·44	414	46·00	464	51·56
15	1·67	65	7·22	115	12·78	165	18·33	215	23·89	265	29·44	315	35·00	365	40·56	415	46·11	465	51·67
16	1·78	66	7·33	116	12·89	166	18·44	216	24·00	266	29·56	316	35·11	366	40·67	416	46·22	466	51·78
17	1·89	67	7·44	117	13·00	167	18·56	217	24·11	267	29·67	317	35·22	367	40·78	417	46·33	467	51·89
18	2·00	68	7·56	118	13·11	168	18·67	218	24·22	268	29·78	318	35·33	368	40·89	418	46·44	468	52·00
19	2·11	69	7·67	119	13·22	169	18·78	219	24·33	269	29·89	319	35·44	369	41·00	419	46·56	469	52·11
20	2·22	70	7·78	120	13·33	170	18·89	220	24·44	270	30·00	320	35·56	370	41·11	420	46·67	470	52·22
21	2·33	71	7·89	121	13·44	171	19·00	221	24·56	271	30·11	321	35·67	371	41·22	421	46·78	471	52·33
22	2·44	72	8·00	122	13·56	172	19·11	222	24·67	272	30·22	322	35·78	372	41·33	422	46·89	472	52·44
23	2·56	73	8·11	123	13·67	173	19·22	223	24·78	273	30·33	323	35·89	373	41·44	423	47·00	473	52·56
24	2·67	74	8·22	124	13·78	174	19·33	224	24·89	274	30·44	324	36·00	374	41·56	424	47·11	474	52·67
25	2·78	75	8·33	125	13·89	175	19·44	225	25·00	275	30·56	325	36·11	375	41·67	425	47·22	475	52·78
26	2·89	76	8·44	126	14·00	176	19·56	226	25·11	276	30·67	326	36·22	376	41·78	426	47·33	476	52·89
27	3·00	77	8·56	127	14·11	177	19·67	227	25·22	277	30·78	327	36·33	377	41·89	427	47·44	477	53·00
28	3·11	78	8·67	128	14·22	178	19·78	228	25·33	278	30·89	328	36·44	378	42·00	428	47·56	478	53·11
29	3·22	79	8·78	129	14·33	179	19·89	229	25·44	279	31·00	329	36·56	379	42·11	429	47·67	479	53·22
30	3·33	80	8·89	130	14·44	180	20·00	230	25·56	280	31·11	330	36·67	380	42·22	430	47·78	480	53·33
31	3·44	81	9·00	131	14·56	181	20·11	231	25·67	281	31·22	331	36·78	381	42·33	431	47·89	481	53·44
32	3·56	82	9·11	132	14·67	182	20·22	232	25·78	282	31·33	332	36·89	382	42·44	432	48·00	482	53·56
33	3·67	83	9·22	133	14·78	183	20·33	233	25·89	283	31·44	333	37·00	383	42·56	433	48·11	483	53·67
34	3·78	84	9·33	134	14·89	184	20·44	234	26·00	284	31·56	334	37·11	384	42·67	434	48·22	484	53·78
35	3·89	85	9·44	135	15·00	185	20·56	235	26·11	285	31·67	335	37·22	385	42·78	435	48·33	485	53·89
36	4·00	86	9·56	136	15·11	186	20·67	236	26·22	286	31·78	336	37·33	386	42·89	436	48·44	486	54·00
37	4·11	87	9·67	137	15·22	187	20·78	237	26·33	287	31·89	337	37·44	387	43·00	437	48·56	487	54·11
38	4·22	88	9·78	138	15·33	188	20·89	238	26·44	288	32·00	338	37·56	388	43·11	438	48·67	488	54·22
39	4·33	89	9·89	139	15·44	189	21·00	239	26·56	289	32·11	339	37·67	389	43·22	439	48·78	489	54·33
40	4·44	90	10·00	140	15·56	190	21·11	240	26·67	290	32·22	340	37·78	390	43·33	440	48·89	490	54·44
41	4·56	91	10·11	141	15·67	191	21·22	241	26·78	291	32·33	341	37·89	391	43·44	441	49·00	491	54·56
42	4·67	92	10·22	142	15·78	192	21·33	242	26·89	292	32·44	342	38·00	392	43·56	442	49·11	492	54·67
43	4·78	93	10·33	143	15·89	193	21·44	243	27·00	293	32·56	343	38·11	393	43·67	443	49·22	493	54·78
44	4·89	94	10·44	144	16·00	194	21·56	244	27·11	294	32·67	344	38·22	394	43·78	444	49·33	494	54·89
45	5·00	95	10·56	145	16·11	195	21·67	245	27·22	295	32·78	345	38·33	395	43·89	445	49·44	495	55·00
46	5·11	96	10·67	146	16·22	196	21·78	246	27·33	296	32·89	346	38·44	396	44·00	446	49·56	496	55·11
47	5·22	97	10·78	147	16·33	197	21·89	247	27·44	297	33·00	347	38·56	397	44·11	447	49·67	497	55·22
48	5·33	98	10·89	148	16·44	198	22·00	248	27·56	298	33·11	348	38·67	398	44·22	448	49·78	498	55·33
49	5·44	99	11·00	149	16·56	199	22·11	249	27·67	299	33·22	349	38·78	399	44·33	449	49·89	499	55·44
50	5·56	100	11·11	150	16·67	200	22·22	250	27·78	300	33·33	350	38·89	400	44·44	450	50·00	500	55·56

On Tax	£1,000 £111	£1,500 £167	£2,000 £222	£2,500 £278	£3,000 £333	£3,500 £389	£4,000 £444	£4,500 £500	£5,000 £556

Note: Dividend income treated as top slice of income and is subject to tax at 10% for starting and basic rate tax payers (page 4) and 32·5% for higher rate taxpayers (pages 10–11).

32·5%   Dividend Tax Credits

£ or p	Tax £ or p	£ or p	Tax £ or p	£	Tax £	£	Tax £	£	Tax £	£	Tax £	£	Tax £	£	Tax £	£	Tax £	£	Tax £
1	0.48	51	24.56	101	48.63	151	72.70	201	96.78	251	120.85	301	144.93	351	169.00	401	193.07	451	217.15
2	0.96	52	25.04	102	49.11	152	73.19	202	97.26	252	121.33	302	145.41	352	169.48	402	193.56	452	217.63
3	1.44	53	25.52	103	49.59	153	73.67	203	97.74	253	121.81	303	145.89	353	169.96	403	194.04	453	218.11
4	1.93	54	26.00	104	50.07	154	74.15	204	98.22	254	122.30	304	146.37	354	170.44	404	194.52	454	218.59
5	2.41	55	26.48	105	50.56	155	74.63	205	98.70	255	122.78	305	146.85	355	170.93	405	195.00	455	219.07
6	2.89	56	26.96	106	51.04	156	75.11	206	99.19	256	123.26	306	147.33	356	171.41	406	195.48	456	219.56
7	3.37	57	27.44	107	51.52	157	75.59	207	99.67	257	123.74	307	147.81	357	171.89	407	195.96	457	220.04
8	3.85	58	27.93	108	52.00	158	76.07	208	100.15	258	124.22	308	148.30	358	172.37	408	196.44	458	220.52
9	4.33	59	28.41	109	52.48	159	76.56	209	100.63	259	124.70	309	148.78	359	172.85	409	196.93	459	221.00
10	4.81	60	28.89	110	52.96	160	77.04	210	101.11	260	125.19	310	149.26	360	173.33	410	197.41	460	221.48
11	5.30	61	29.37	111	53.44	161	77.52	211	101.59	261	125.67	311	149.74	361	173.81	411	197.89	461	221.96
12	5.78	62	29.85	112	53.93	162	78.00	212	102.07	262	126.15	312	150.22	362	174.30	412	198.37	462	222.44
13	6.26	63	30.33	113	54.41	163	78.48	213	102.56	263	126.63	313	150.70	363	174.78	413	198.85	463	222.93
14	6.74	64	30.81	114	54.89	164	78.96	214	103.04	264	127.11	314	151.19	364	175.26	414	199.33	464	223.41
15	7.22	65	31.30	115	55.37	165	79.44	215	103.52	265	127.59	315	151.67	365	175.74	415	199.81	465	223.89
16	7.70	66	31.78	116	55.85	166	79.93	216	104.00	266	128.07	316	152.15	366	176.22	416	200.30	466	224.37
17	8.19	67	32.26	117	56.33	167	80.41	217	104.48	267	128.56	317	152.63	367	176.70	417	200.78	467	224.85
18	8.67	68	32.74	118	56.81	168	80.89	218	104.96	268	129.04	318	153.11	368	177.19	418	201.26	468	225.33
19	9.15	69	33.22	119	57.30	169	81.37	219	105.44	269	129.52	319	153.59	369	177.67	419	201.74	469	225.81
20	9.63	70	33.70	120	57.78	170	81.85	220	105.93	270	130.00	320	154.07	370	178.15	420	202.22	470	226.30
21	10.11	71	34.19	121	58.26	171	82.33	221	106.41	271	130.48	321	154.56	371	178.63	421	202.70	471	226.78
22	10.59	72	34.67	122	58.74	172	82.81	222	106.89	272	130.96	322	155.04	372	179.11	422	203.19	472	227.26
23	11.07	73	35.15	123	59.22	173	83.30	223	107.37	273	131.44	323	155.52	373	179.59	423	203.67	473	227.74
24	11.56	74	35.63	124	59.70	174	83.78	224	107.85	274	131.93	324	156.00	374	180.07	424	204.15	474	228.22
25	12.04	75	36.11	125	60.19	175	84.26	225	108.33	275	132.41	325	156.48	375	180.56	425	204.63	475	228.70
26	12.52	76	36.59	126	60.67	176	84.74	226	108.81	276	132.89	326	156.96	376	181.04	426	205.11	476	229.19
27	13.00	77	37.07	127	61.15	177	85.22	227	109.30	277	133.37	327	157.44	377	181.52	427	205.59	477	229.67
28	13.48	78	37.56	128	61.63	178	85.70	228	109.78	278	133.85	328	157.93	378	182.00	428	206.07	478	230.15
29	13.96	79	38.04	129	62.11	179	86.19	229	110.26	279	134.33	329	158.41	379	182.48	429	206.56	479	230.63
30	14.44	80	38.52	130	62.59	180	86.67	230	110.74	280	134.81	330	158.89	380	182.96	430	207.04	480	231.11
31	14.93	81	39.00	131	63.07	181	87.15	231	111.22	281	135.30	331	159.37	381	183.44	431	207.52	481	231.59
32	15.41	82	39.48	132	63.56	182	87.63	232	111.70	282	135.78	332	159.85	382	183.93	432	208.00	482	232.07
33	15.89	83	39.96	133	64.04	183	88.11	233	112.19	283	136.26	333	160.33	383	184.41	433	208.48	483	232.56
34	16.37	84	40.44	134	64.52	184	88.59	234	112.67	284	136.74	334	160.81	384	184.89	434	208.96	484	233.04
35	16.85	85	40.93	135	65.00	185	89.07	235	113.15	285	137.22	335	161.30	385	185.37	435	209.44	485	233.52
36	17.33	86	41.41	136	65.48	186	89.56	236	113.63	286	137.70	336	161.78	386	185.85	436	209.93	486	234.00
37	17.81	87	41.89	137	65.96	187	90.04	237	114.11	287	138.19	337	162.26	387	186.33	437	210.41	487	234.48
38	18.30	88	42.37	138	66.44	188	90.52	238	114.59	288	138.67	338	162.74	388	186.81	438	210.89	488	234.96
39	18.78	89	42.85	139	66.93	189	91.00	239	115.07	289	139.15	339	163.22	389	187.30	439	211.37	489	235.44
40	19.26	90	43.33	140	67.41	190	91.48	240	115.56	290	139.63	340	163.70	390	187.78	440	211.85	490	235.93
41	19.74	91	43.81	141	67.89	191	91.96	241	116.04	291	140.11	341	164.19	391	188.26	441	212.33	491	236.41
42	20.22	92	44.30	142	68.37	192	92.44	242	116.52	292	140.59	342	164.67	392	188.74	442	212.81	492	236.89
43	20.70	93	44.78	143	68.85	193	92.93	243	117.00	293	141.07	343	165.15	393	189.22	443	213.30	493	237.37
44	21.19	94	45.26	144	69.33	194	93.41	244	117.48	294	141.56	344	165.63	394	189.70	444	213.78	494	237.85
45	21.67	95	45.74	145	69.81	195	93.89	245	117.96	295	142.04	345	166.11	395	190.19	445	214.26	495	238.33
46	22.15	96	46.22	146	70.30	196	94.37	246	118.44	296	142.52	346	166.59	396	190.67	446	214.74	496	238.81
47	22.63	97	46.70	147	70.78	197	94.85	247	118.93	297	143.00	347	167.07	397	191.15	447	215.22	497	239.30
48	23.11	98	47.19	148	71.26	198	95.33	248	119.41	298	143.48	348	167.56	398	191.63	448	215.70	498	239.78
49	23.59	99	47.67	149	71.74	199	95.81	249	119.89	299	143.96	349	168.04	399	192.11	449	216.19	499	240.26
50	24.07	100	48.15	150	72.22	200	96.30	250	120.37	300	144.44	350	168.52	400	192.59	450	216.67	500	240.74

On Tax	£1,000 £481	£1,500 £722	£2,000 £963	£2,500 £1,204	£3,000 £1,444	£3,500 £1,685	£4,000 £1,926	£4,500 £2,167	£5,000 £2,407

Dividend Tax Credits   42·5%

£ or p	Tax £ or p	£ or p	Tax £ or p	£	Tax £	£	Tax £	£	Tax £	£	Tax £	£	Tax £	£	Tax £	£	Tax £	£	Tax £
1	0.74	51	37.70	101	74.65	151	111.61	201	148.57	251	185.52	301	222.48	351	259.43	401	296.39	451	333.35
2	1.48	52	38.43	102	75.39	152	112.35	202	149.30	252	186.26	302	223.22	352	260.17	402	297.13	452	334.09
3	2.22	53	39.17	103	76.13	153	113.09	203	150.04	253	187.00	303	223.96	353	260.91	403	297.87	453	334.83
4	2.96	54	39.91	104	76.87	154	113.83	204	150.78	254	187.74	304	224.70	354	261.65	404	298.61	454	335.57
5	3.70	55	40.65	105	77.61	155	114.57	205	151.52	255	188.48	305	225.43	355	262.39	405	299.35	455	336.30
6	4.43	56	41.39	106	78.35	156	115.30	206	152.26	256	189.22	306	226.17	356	263.13	406	300.09	456	337.04
7	5.17	57	42.13	107	79.09	157	116.04	207	153.00	257	189.96	307	226.91	357	263.87	407	300.83	457	337.78
8	5.91	58	42.87	108	79.83	158	116.78	208	153.74	258	190.70	308	227.65	358	264.61	408	301.57	458	338.52
9	6.65	59	43.61	109	80.57	159	117.52	209	154.48	259	191.43	309	228.39	359	265.35	409	302.30	459	339.26
10	7.39	60	44.35	110	81.30	160	118.26	210	155.22	260	192.17	310	229.13	360	266.09	410	303.04	460	340.00
11	8.13	61	45.09	111	82.04	161	119.00	211	155.96	261	192.91	311	229.87	361	266.83	411	303.78	461	340.74
12	8.87	62	45.83	112	82.78	162	119.74	212	156.70	262	193.65	312	230.61	362	267.57	412	304.52	462	341.48
13	9.61	63	46.57	113	83.52	163	120.48	213	157.43	263	194.39	313	231.35	363	268.30	413	305.26	463	342.22
14	10.35	64	47.30	114	84.26	164	121.22	214	158.17	264	195.13	314	232.09	364	269.04	414	306.00	464	342.96
15	11.09	65	48.04	115	85.00	165	121.96	215	158.91	265	195.87	315	232.83	365	269.78	415	306.74	465	343.70
16	11.83	66	48.78	116	85.74	166	122.70	216	159.65	266	196.61	316	233.57	366	270.52	416	307.48	466	344.43
17	12.57	67	49.52	117	86.48	167	123.43	217	160.39	267	197.35	317	234.30	367	271.26	417	308.22	467	345.17
18	13.30	68	50.26	118	87.22	168	124.17	218	161.13	268	198.09	318	235.04	368	272.00	418	308.96	468	345.91
19	14.04	69	51.00	119	87.96	169	124.91	219	161.87	269	198.83	319	235.78	369	272.74	419	309.70	469	346.65
20	14.78	70	51.74	120	88.70	170	125.65	220	162.61	270	199.57	320	236.52	370	273.48	420	310.43	470	347.39
21	15.52	71	52.48	121	89.43	171	126.39	221	163.35	271	200.30	321	237.26	371	274.22	421	311.17	471	348.13
22	16.26	72	53.22	122	90.17	172	127.13	222	164.09	272	201.04	322	238.00	372	274.96	422	311.91	472	348.87
23	17.00	73	53.96	123	90.91	173	127.87	223	164.83	273	201.78	323	238.74	373	275.70	423	312.65	473	349.61
24	17.74	74	54.70	124	91.65	174	128.61	224	165.57	274	202.52	324	239.48	374	276.43	424	313.39	474	350.35
25	18.48	75	55.43	125	92.39	175	129.35	225	166.30	275	203.26	325	240.22	375	277.17	425	314.13	475	351.09
26	19.22	76	56.17	126	93.13	176	130.09	226	167.04	276	204.00	326	240.96	376	277.91	426	314.87	476	351.83
27	19.96	77	56.91	127	93.87	177	130.83	227	167.78	277	204.74	327	241.70	377	278.65	427	315.61	477	352.57
28	20.70	78	57.65	128	94.61	178	131.57	228	168.52	278	205.48	328	242.43	378	279.39	428	316.35	478	353.30
29	21.43	79	58.39	129	95.35	179	132.30	229	169.26	279	206.22	329	243.17	379	280.13	429	317.09	479	354.04
30	22.17	80	59.13	130	96.09	180	133.04	230	170.00	280	206.96	330	243.91	380	280.87	430	317.83	480	354.78
31	22.91	81	59.87	131	96.83	181	133.78	231	170.74	281	207.70	331	244.65	381	281.61	431	318.57	481	355.52
32	23.65	82	60.61	132	97.57	182	134.52	232	171.48	282	208.43	332	245.39	382	282.35	432	319.30	482	356.26
33	24.39	83	61.35	133	98.30	183	135.26	233	172.22	283	209.17	333	246.13	383	283.09	433	320.04	483	357.00
34	25.13	84	62.09	134	99.04	184	136.00	234	172.96	284	209.91	334	246.87	384	283.83	434	320.78	484	357.74
35	25.87	85	62.83	135	99.78	185	136.74	235	173.70	285	210.65	335	247.61	385	284.57	435	321.52	485	358.48
36	26.61	86	63.57	136	100.52	186	137.48	236	174.43	286	211.39	336	248.35	386	285.30	436	322.26	486	359.22
37	27.35	87	64.30	137	101.26	187	138.22	237	175.17	287	212.13	337	249.09	387	286.04	437	323.00	487	359.96
38	28.09	88	65.04	138	102.00	188	138.96	238	175.91	288	212.87	338	249.83	388	286.78	438	323.74	488	360.70
39	28.83	89	65.78	139	102.74	189	139.70	239	176.65	289	213.61	339	250.57	389	287.52	439	324.48	489	361.43
40	29.57	90	66.52	140	103.48	190	140.43	240	177.39	290	214.35	340	251.30	390	288.26	440	325.22	490	362.17
41	30.30	91	67.26	141	104.22	191	141.17	241	178.13	291	215.09	341	252.04	391	289.00	441	325.96	491	362.91
42	31.04	92	68.00	142	104.96	192	141.91	242	178.87	292	215.83	342	252.78	392	289.74	442	326.70	492	363.65
43	31.78	93	68.74	143	105.70	193	142.65	243	179.61	293	216.57	343	253.52	393	290.48	443	327.43	493	364.39
44	32.52	94	69.48	144	106.43	194	143.39	244	180.35	294	217.30	344	254.26	394	291.22	444	328.17	494	365.13
45	33.26	95	70.22	145	107.17	195	144.13	245	181.09	295	218.04	345	255.00	395	291.96	445	328.91	495	365.87
46	34.00	96	70.96	146	107.91	196	144.87	246	181.83	296	218.78	346	255.74	396	292.70	446	329.65	496	366.61
47	34.74	97	71.70	147	108.65	197	145.61	247	182.57	297	219.52	347	256.48	397	293.43	447	330.39	497	367.35
48	35.48	98	72.43	148	109.39	198	146.35	248	183.30	298	220.26	348	257.22	398	294.17	448	331.13	498	368.09
49	36.22	99	73.17	149	110.13	199	147.09	249	184.04	299	221.00	349	257.96	399	294.91	449	331.87	499	368.83
50	36.96	100	73.91	150	110.87	200	147.83	250	184.78	300	221.74	350	258.70	400	295.65	450	332.61	500	369.57

On Tax	£1,000 £739	£1,500 £1,109	£2,000 £1,478	£2,500 £1,848	£3,000 £2,217	£3,500 £2,587	£4,000 £2,957	£4,500 £3,326	£5,000 £3,696

20% VAT at Standard Rate

£ or p	Tax £ or p	£ or p	Tax £ or p	£	Tax £	£	Tax £	£	Tax £	£	Tax £	£	Tax £	£	Tax £	£	Tax £	£	Tax £
1	0·20	51	10·20	101	20·20	151	30·20	201	40·20	251	50·20	301	60·20	351	70·20	401	80·20	451	90·20
2	0·40	52	10·40	102	20·40	152	30·40	202	40·40	252	50·40	302	60·40	352	70·40	402	80·40	452	90·40
3	0·60	53	10·60	103	20·60	153	30·60	203	40·60	253	50·60	303	60·60	353	70·60	403	80·60	453	90·60
4	0·80	54	10·80	104	20·80	154	30·80	204	40·80	254	50·80	304	60·80	354	70·80	404	80·80	454	90·80
5	1·00	55	11·00	105	21·00	155	31·00	205	41·00	255	51·00	305	61·00	355	71·00	405	81·00	455	91·00
6	1·20	56	11·20	106	21·20	156	31·20	206	41·20	256	51·20	306	61·20	356	71·20	406	81·20	456	91·20
7	1·40	57	11·40	107	21·40	157	31·40	207	41·40	257	51·40	307	61·40	357	71·40	407	81·40	457	91·40
8	1·60	58	11·60	108	21·60	158	31·60	208	41·60	258	51·60	308	61·60	358	71·60	408	81·60	458	91·60
9	1·80	59	11·80	109	21·80	159	31·80	209	41·80	259	51·80	309	61·80	359	71·80	409	81·80	459	91·80
10	2·00	60	12·00	110	22·00	160	32·00	210	42·00	260	52·00	310	62·00	360	72·00	410	82·00	460	92·00
11	2·20	61	12·20	111	22·20	161	32·20	211	42·20	261	52·20	311	62·20	361	72·20	411	82·20	461	92·20
12	2·40	62	12·40	112	22·40	162	32·40	212	42·40	262	52·40	312	62·40	362	72·40	412	82·40	462	92·40
13	2·60	63	12·60	113	22·60	163	32·60	213	42·60	263	52·60	313	62·60	363	72·60	413	82·60	463	92·60
14	2·80	64	12·80	114	22·80	164	32·80	214	42·80	264	52·80	314	62·80	364	72·80	414	82·80	464	92·80
15	3·00	65	13·00	115	23·00	165	33·00	215	43·00	265	53·00	315	63·00	365	73·00	415	83·00	465	93·00
16	3·20	66	13·20	116	23·20	166	33·20	216	43·20	266	53·20	316	63·20	366	73·20	416	83·20	466	93·20
17	3·40	67	13·40	117	23·40	167	33·40	217	43·40	267	53·40	317	63·40	367	73·40	417	83·40	467	93·40
18	3·60	68	13·60	118	23·60	168	33·60	218	43·60	268	53·60	318	63·60	368	73·60	418	83·60	468	93·60
19	3·80	69	13·80	119	23·80	169	33·80	219	43·80	269	53·80	319	63·80	369	73·80	419	83·80	469	93·80
20	4·00	70	14·00	120	24·00	170	34·00	220	44·00	270	54·00	320	64·00	370	74·00	420	84·00	470	94·00
21	4·20	71	14·20	121	24·20	171	34·20	221	44·20	271	54·20	321	64·20	371	74·20	421	84·20	471	94·20
22	4·40	72	14·40	122	24·40	172	34·40	222	44·40	272	54·40	322	64·40	372	74·40	422	84·40	472	94·40
23	4·60	73	14·60	123	24·60	173	34·60	223	44·60	273	54·60	323	64·60	373	74·60	423	84·60	473	94·60
24	4·80	74	14·80	124	24·80	174	34·80	224	44·80	274	54·80	324	64·80	374	74·80	424	84·80	474	94·80
25	5·00	75	15·00	125	25·00	175	35·00	225	45·00	275	55·00	325	65·00	375	75·00	425	85·00	475	95·00
26	5·20	76	15·20	126	25·20	176	35·20	226	45·20	276	55·20	326	65·20	376	75·20	426	85·20	476	95·20
27	5·40	77	15·40	127	25·40	177	35·40	227	45·40	277	55·40	327	65·40	377	75·40	427	85·40	477	95·40
28	5·60	78	15·60	128	25·60	178	35·60	228	45·60	278	55·60	328	65·60	378	75·60	428	85·60	478	95·60
29	5·80	79	15·80	129	25·80	179	35·80	229	45·80	279	55·80	329	65·80	379	75·80	429	85·80	479	95·80
30	6·00	80	16·00	130	26·00	180	36·00	230	46·00	280	56·00	330	66·00	380	76·00	430	86·00	480	96·00
31	6·20	81	16·20	131	26·20	181	36·20	231	46·20	281	56·20	331	66·20	381	76·20	431	86·20	481	96·20
32	6·40	82	16·40	132	26·40	182	36·40	232	46·40	282	56·40	332	66·40	382	76·40	432	86·40	482	96·40
33	6·60	83	16·60	133	26·60	183	36·60	233	46·60	283	56·60	333	66·60	383	76·60	433	86·60	483	96·60
34	6·80	84	16·80	134	26·80	184	36·80	234	46·80	284	56·80	334	66·80	384	76·80	434	86·80	484	96·80
35	7·00	85	17·00	135	27·00	185	37·00	235	47·00	285	57·00	335	67·00	385	77·00	435	87·00	485	97·00
36	7·20	86	17·20	136	27·20	186	37·20	236	47·20	286	57·20	336	67·20	386	77·20	436	87·20	486	97·20
37	7·40	87	17·40	137	27·40	187	37·40	237	47·40	287	57·40	337	67·40	387	77·40	437	87·40	487	97·40
38	7·60	88	17·60	138	27·60	188	37·60	238	47·60	288	57·60	338	67·60	388	77·60	438	87·60	488	97·60
39	7·80	89	17·80	139	27·80	189	37·80	239	47·80	289	57·80	339	67·80	389	77·80	439	87·80	489	97·80
40	8·00	90	18·00	140	28·00	190	38·00	240	48·00	290	58·00	340	68·00	390	78·00	440	88·00	490	98·00
41	8·20	91	18·20	141	28·20	191	38·20	241	48·20	291	58·20	341	68·20	391	78·20	441	88·20	491	98·20
42	8·40	92	18·40	142	28·40	192	38·40	242	48·40	292	58·40	342	68·40	392	78·40	442	88·40	492	98·40
43	8·60	93	18·60	143	28·60	193	38·60	243	48·60	293	58·60	343	68·60	393	78·60	443	88·60	493	98·60
44	8·80	94	18·80	144	28·80	194	38·80	244	48·80	294	58·80	344	68·80	394	78·80	444	88·80	494	98·80
45	9·00	95	19·00	145	29·00	195	39·00	245	49·00	295	59·00	345	69·00	395	79·00	445	89·00	495	99·00
46	9·20	96	19·20	146	29·20	196	39·20	246	49·20	296	59·20	346	69·20	396	79·20	446	89·20	496	99·20
47	9·40	97	19·40	147	29·40	197	39·40	247	49·40	297	59·40	347	69·40	397	79·40	447	89·40	497	99·40
48	9·60	98	19·60	148	29·60	198	39·60	248	49·60	298	59·60	348	69·60	398	79·60	448	89·60	498	99·60
49	9·80	99	19·80	149	29·80	199	39·80	249	49·80	299	59·80	349	69·80	399	79·80	449	89·80	499	99·80
50	10·00	100	20·00	150	30·00	200	40·00	250	50·00	300	60·00	350	70·00	400	80·00	450	90·00	500	100·00

| On | | £1,000 | | £1,500 | | £2,000 | | £2,500 | | £3,000 | | £3,500 | | £4,000 | | £4,500 | | £5,000 | |
| Tax | | £200 | | £300 | | £400 | | £500 | | £600 | | £700 | | £800 | | £900 | | £1,000 | |

VAT Content of Inclusive Prices 20·0%

Inclusive Price £ or p	VAT @20% £ or p	Basic Price £ or p	Inclusive Price £ or p	VAT @20% £ or p	Basic Price £ or p	Inclusive Price £ or p	VAT @20% £ or p	Basic Price £ or p	Inclusive Price £ or p	VAT @20% £ or p	Basic Price £ or p	Inclusive Price £ or p	VAT @20% £ or p	Basic Price £ or p	Inclusive Price £ or p	VAT @20% £ or p	Basic Price £ or p
1	0·17	0·83	51	8·50	42·50	101	16·83	84·17	151	25·17	125·83	201	33·50	167·50	251	41·83	209·17
2	0·33	1·67	52	8·67	43·33	102	17·00	85·00	152	25·33	126·67	202	33·67	168·33	252	42·00	210·00
3	0·50	2·50	53	8·83	44·17	103	17·17	85·83	153	25·50	127·50	203	33·83	169·17	253	42·17	210·83
4	0·67	3·33	54	9·00	45·00	104	17·33	86·67	154	25·67	128·33	204	34·00	170·00	254	42·33	211·67
5	0·83	4·17	55	9·17	45·83	105	17·50	87·50	155	25·83	129·17	205	34·17	170·83	255	42·50	212·50
6	1·00	5·00	56	9·33	46·67	106	17·67	88·33	156	26·00	130·00	206	34·33	171·67	256	42·67	213·33
7	1·17	5·83	57	9·50	47·50	107	17·83	89·17	157	26·17	130·83	207	34·50	172·50	257	42·83	214·17
8	1·33	6·67	58	9·67	48·33	108	18·00	90·00	158	26·33	131·67	208	34·67	173·33	258	43·00	215·00
9	1·50	7·50	59	9·83	49·17	109	18·17	90·83	159	26·50	132·50	209	34·83	174·17	259	43·17	215·83
10	1·67	8·33	60	10·00	50·00	110	18·33	91·67	160	26·67	133·33	210	35·00	175·00	260	43·33	216·67
11	1·83	9·17	61	10·17	50·83	111	18·50	92·50	161	26·83	134·17	211	35·17	175·83	261	43·50	217·50
12	2·00	10·00	62	10·33	51·67	112	18·67	93·33	162	27·00	135·00	212	35·33	176·67	262	43·67	218·33
13	2·17	10·83	63	10·50	52·50	113	18·83	94·17	163	27·17	135·83	213	35·50	177·50	263	43·83	219·17
14	2·33	11·67	64	10·67	53·33	114	19·00	95·00	164	27·33	136·67	214	35·67	178·33	264	44·00	220·00
15	2·50	12·50	65	10·83	54·17	115	19·17	95·83	165	27·50	137·50	215	35·83	179·17	265	44·17	220·83
16	2·67	13·33	66	11·00	55·00	116	19·33	96·67	166	27·67	138·33	216	36·00	180·00	266	44·33	221·67
17	2·83	14·17	67	11·17	55·83	117	19·50	97·50	167	27·83	139·17	217	36·17	180·83	267	44·50	222·50
18	3·00	15·00	68	11·33	56·67	118	19·67	98·33	168	28·00	140·00	218	36·33	181·67	268	44·67	223·33
19	3·17	15·83	69	11·50	57·50	119	19·83	99·17	169	28·17	140·83	219	36·50	182·50	269	44·83	224·17
20	3·33	16·67	70	11·67	58·33	120	20·00	100·00	170	28·33	141·67	220	36·67	183·33	270	45·00	225·00
21	3·50	17·50	71	11·83	59·17	121	20·17	100·83	171	28·50	142·50	221	36·83	184·17	271	45·17	225·83
22	3·67	18·33	72	12·00	60·00	122	20·33	101·67	172	28·67	143·33	222	37·00	185·00	272	45·33	226·67
23	3·83	19·17	73	12·17	60·83	123	20·50	102·50	173	28·83	144·17	223	37·17	185·83	273	45·50	227·50
24	4·00	20·00	74	12·33	61·67	124	20·67	103·33	174	29·00	145·00	224	37·33	186·67	274	45·67	228·33
25	4·17	20·83	75	12·50	62·50	125	20·83	104·17	175	29·17	145·83	225	37·50	187·50	275	45·83	229·17
26	4·33	21·67	76	12·67	63·33	126	21·00	105·00	176	29·33	146·67	226	37·67	188·33	276	46·00	230·00
27	4·50	22·50	77	12·83	64·17	127	21·17	105·83	177	29·50	147·50	227	37·83	189·17	277	46·17	230·83
28	4·67	23·33	78	13·00	65·00	128	21·33	106·67	178	29·67	148·33	228	38·00	190·00	278	46·33	231·67
29	4·83	24·17	79	13·17	65·83	129	21·50	107·50	179	29·83	149·17	229	38·17	190·83	279	46·50	232·50
30	5·00	25·00	80	13·33	66·67	130	21·67	108·33	180	30·00	150·00	230	38·33	191·67	280	46·67	233·33
31	5·17	25·83	81	13·50	67·50	131	21·83	109·17	181	30·17	150·83	231	38·50	192·50	281	46·83	234·17
32	5·33	26·67	82	13·67	68·33	132	22·00	110·00	182	30·33	151·67	232	38·67	193·33	282	47·00	235·00
33	5·50	27·50	83	13·83	69·17	133	22·17	110·83	183	30·50	152·50	233	38·83	194·17	283	47·17	235·83
34	5·67	28·33	84	14·00	70·00	134	22·33	111·67	184	30·67	153·33	234	39·00	195·00	284	47·33	236·67
35	5·83	29·17	85	14·17	70·83	135	22·50	112·50	185	30·83	154·17	235	39·17	195·83	285	47·50	237·50
36	6·00	30·00	86	14·33	71·67	136	22·67	113·33	186	31·00	155·00	236	39·33	196·67	286	47·67	238·33
37	6·17	30·83	87	14·50	72·50	137	22·83	114·17	187	31·17	155·83	237	39·50	197·50	287	47·83	239·17
38	6·33	31·67	88	14·67	73·33	138	23·00	115·00	188	31·33	156·67	238	39·67	198·33	288	48·00	240·00
39	6·50	32·50	89	14·83	74·17	139	23·17	115·83	189	31·50	157·50	239	39·83	199·17	289	48·17	240·83
40	6·67	33·33	90	15·00	75·00	140	23·33	116·67	190	31·67	158·33	240	40·00	200·00	290	48·33	241·67
41	6·83	34·17	91	15·17	75·83	141	23·50	117·50	191	31·83	159·17	241	40·17	200·83	291	48·50	242·50
42	7·00	35·00	92	15·33	76·67	142	23·67	118·33	192	32·00	160·00	242	40·33	201·67	292	48·67	243·33
43	7·17	35·83	93	15·50	77·50	143	23·83	119·17	193	32·17	160·83	243	40·50	202·50	293	48·83	244·17
44	7·33	36·67	94	15·67	78·33	144	24·00	120·00	194	32·33	161·67	244	40·67	203·33	294	49·00	245·00
45	7·50	37·50	95	15·83	79·17	145	24·17	120·83	195	32·50	162·50	245	40·83	204·17	295	49·17	245·83
46	7·67	38·33	96	16·00	80·00	146	24·33	121·67	196	32·67	163·33	246	41·00	205·00	296	49·33	246·67
47	7·83	39·17	97	16·17	80·83	147	24·50	122·50	197	32·83	164·17	247	41·17	205·83	297	49·50	247·50
48	8·00	40·00	98	16·33	81·67	148	24·67	123·33	198	33·00	165·00	248	41·33	206·67	298	49·67	248·33
49	8·17	40·83	99	16·50	82·50	149	24·83	124·17	199	33·17	165·83	249	41·50	207·50	299	49·83	249·17
50	8·33	41·67	100	16·67	83·33	150	25·00	125·00	200	33·33	166·67	250	41·67	208·33	300	50·00	250·00
500	83·33	416·67	600	100·00	500·00	700	116·67	583·33	800	133·33	666·67	900	150·00	750·00	1,000	166·67	833·33

Number of days Table: Tax Year

Years other than leap years

(Quarter days are highlighted)

Days	April lapsed	April to go	May lapsed	May to go	June lapsed	June to go	July lapsed	July to go	August lapsed	August to go	September lapsed	September to go	October lapsed	October to go	November lapsed	November to go	December lapsed	December to go	January lapsed	January to go	February lapsed	February to go	March lapsed	March to go	Days
1	361	4	26	339	57	308	87	278	118	247	149	216	179	186	210	155	240	125	271	94	302	63	330	35	1
2	362	3	27	338	58	307	88	277	119	246	150	215	180	185	211	154	241	124	272	93	303	62	331	34	2
3	363	2	28	337	59	306	89	276	120	245	151	214	181	184	212	153	242	123	273	92	304	61	332	33	3
4	364	1	29	336	60	305	90	275	121	244	152	213	182	183	213	152	243	122	274	91	305	60	333	32	4
5	365	0	30	335	61	304	91	274	122	243	153	212	183	182	214	151	244	121	275	90	306	59	334	31	5
6	1	364	31	334	62	303	92	273	123	242	154	211	184	181	215	150	245	120	276	89	307	58	335	30	6
7	2	363	32	333	63	302	93	272	124	241	155	210	185	180	216	149	246	119	277	88	308	57	336	29	7
8	3	362	33	332	64	301	94	271	125	240	156	209	186	179	217	148	247	118	278	87	309	56	337	28	8
9	4	361	34	331	65	300	95	270	126	239	157	208	187	178	218	147	248	117	279	86	310	55	338	27	9
10	5	360	35	330	66	299	96	269	127	238	158	207	188	177	219	146	249	116	280	85	311	54	339	26	10
11	6	359	36	329	67	298	97	268	128	237	159	206	189	176	220	145	250	115	281	84	312	53	340	25	11
12	7	358	37	328	68	297	98	267	129	236	160	205	190	175	221	144	251	114	282	83	313	52	341	24	12
13	8	357	38	327	69	296	99	266	130	235	161	204	191	174	222	143	252	113	283	82	314	51	342	23	13
14	9	356	39	326	70	295	100	265	131	234	162	203	192	173	223	142	253	112	284	81	315	50	343	22	14
15	10	355	40	325	71	294	101	264	132	233	163	202	193	172	224	141	254	111	285	80	316	49	344	21	15
16	11	354	41	324	72	293	102	263	133	232	164	201	194	171	225	140	255	110	286	79	317	48	345	20	16
17	12	353	42	323	73	292	103	262	134	231	165	200	195	170	226	139	256	109	287	78	318	47	346	19	17
18	13	352	43	322	74	291	104	261	135	230	166	199	196	169	227	138	257	108	288	77	319	46	347	18	18
19	14	351	44	321	75	290	105	260	136	229	167	198	197	168	228	137	258	107	289	76	320	45	348	17	19
20	15	350	45	320	76	289	106	259	137	228	168	197	198	167	229	136	259	106	290	75	321	44	349	16	20
21	16	349	46	319	77	288	107	258	138	227	169	196	199	166	230	135	260	105	291	74	322	43	350	15	21
22	17	348	47	318	78	287	108	257	139	226	170	195	200	165	231	134	261	104	292	73	323	42	351	14	22
23	18	347	48	317	79	286	109	256	140	225	171	194	201	164	232	133	262	103	293	72	324	41	352	13	23
24	19	346	49	316	80	285	110	255	141	224	172	193	202	163	233	132	263	102	294	71	325	40	353	12	24
25	20	345	50	315	81	284	111	254	142	223	173	192	203	162	234	131	264	101	295	70	326	39	354	11	25
26	21	344	51	314	82	283	112	253	143	222	174	191	204	161	235	130	265	100	296	69	327	38	355	10	26
27	22	343	52	313	83	282	113	252	144	221	175	190	205	160	236	129	266	99	297	68	328	37	356	9	27
28	23	342	53	312	84	281	114	251	145	220	176	189	206	159	237	128	267	98	298	67	329	36	357	8	28
29	24	341	54	311	85	280	115	250	146	219	177	188	207	158	238	127	268	97	299	66			358	7	29
30	25	340	55	310	86	279	116	249	147	218	178	187	208	157	239	126	269	96	300	65			359	6	30
31			56	309			117	248	148	217			209	156			270	95	301	64			360	5	31

Leap years falling within tax years 2011/12   2015/16   2019/2020

(Quarter days are highlighted)

Days	April lapsed	April to go	May lapsed	May to go	June lapsed	June to go	July lapsed	July to go	August lapsed	August to go	September lapsed	September to go	October lapsed	October to go	November lapsed	November to go	December lapsed	December to go	January lapsed	January to go	February lapsed	February to go	March lapsed	March to go	Days
1	362	4	26	340	57	309	87	279	118	248	149	217	179	187	210	156	240	126	271	95	302	64	331	35	1
2	363	3	27	339	58	308	88	278	119	247	150	216	180	186	211	155	241	125	272	94	303	63	332	34	2
3	364	2	28	338	59	307	89	277	120	246	151	215	181	185	212	154	242	124	273	93	304	62	333	33	3
4	365	1	29	337	60	306	90	276	121	245	152	214	182	184	213	153	243	123	274	92	305	61	334	32	4
5	366	0	30	336	61	305	91	275	122	244	153	213	183	183	214	152	244	122	275	91	306	60	335	31	5
6	1	365	31	335	62	304	92	274	123	243	154	212	184	182	215	151	245	121	276	90	307	59	336	30	6
7	2	364	32	334	63	303	93	273	124	242	155	211	185	181	216	150	246	120	277	89	308	58	337	29	7
8	3	363	33	333	64	302	94	272	125	241	156	210	186	180	217	149	247	119	278	88	309	57	338	28	8
9	4	362	34	332	65	301	95	271	126	240	157	209	187	179	218	148	248	118	279	87	310	56	339	27	9
10	5	361	35	331	66	300	96	270	127	239	158	208	188	178	219	147	249	117	280	86	311	55	340	26	10
11	6	360	36	330	67	299	97	269	128	238	159	207	189	177	220	146	250	116	281	85	312	54	341	25	11
12	7	359	37	329	68	298	98	268	129	237	160	206	190	176	221	145	251	115	282	84	313	53	342	24	12
13	8	358	38	328	69	297	99	267	130	236	161	205	191	175	222	144	252	114	283	83	314	52	343	23	13
14	9	357	39	327	70	296	100	266	131	235	162	204	192	174	223	143	253	113	284	82	315	51	344	22	14
15	10	356	40	326	71	295	101	265	132	234	163	203	193	173	224	142	254	112	285	81	316	50	345	21	15
16	11	355	41	325	72	294	102	264	133	233	164	202	194	172	225	141	255	111	286	80	317	49	346	20	16
17	12	354	42	324	73	293	103	263	134	232	165	201	195	171	226	140	256	110	287	79	318	48	347	19	17
18	13	353	43	323	74	292	104	262	135	231	166	200	196	170	227	139	257	109	288	78	319	47	348	18	18
19	14	352	44	322	75	291	105	261	136	230	167	199	197	169	228	138	258	108	289	77	320	46	349	17	19
20	15	351	45	321	76	290	106	260	137	229	168	198	198	168	229	137	259	107	290	76	321	45	350	16	20
21	16	350	46	320	77	289	107	259	138	228	169	197	199	167	230	136	260	106	291	75	322	44	351	15	21
22	17	349	47	319	78	288	108	258	139	227	170	196	200	166	231	135	261	105	292	74	323	43	352	14	22
23	18	348	48	318	79	287	109	257	140	226	171	195	201	165	232	134	262	104	293	73	324	42	353	13	23
24	19	347	49	317	80	286	110	256	141	225	172	194	202	164	233	133	263	103	294	72	325	41	354	12	24
25	20	346	50	316	81	285	111	255	142	224	173	193	203	163	234	132	264	102	295	71	326	40	355	11	25
26	21	345	51	315	82	284	112	254	143	223	174	192	204	162	235	131	265	101	296	70	327	39	356	10	26
27	22	344	52	314	83	283	113	253	144	222	175	191	205	161	236	130	266	100	297	69	328	38	357	9	27
28	23	343	53	313	84	282	114	252	145	221	176	190	206	150	237	129	267	99	298	68	329	37	358	8	28
29	24	342	54	312	85	281	115	251	146	220	177	189	207	159	238	128	268	98	299	67	330	36	359	7	29
30	25	341	55	311	86	280	116	250	147	219	178	188	208	158	239	127	269	97	300	66			360	6	30
31			56	310			117	249	148	218			209	157			270	96	301	65			361	5	31

Tax Year Planner 2012/13

	April	May	June	July	August	Sept	Oct	Nov	Dec	Jan	Feb	March	April	
Mon							1						1	Mon
Tue		1					2			1			2	Tue
Wed		2		1			3			2			3	Wed
Thurs		3			2		4	1		3			4	Thurs
Fri		4	1		3		5	2		4	1	1	5	Fri
Sat		5	2		4	1	6	3	1	5	2	2	6	Sat
Sun	1	6	3	1	5	2	7	4	2	6	3	3	7	Sun
Mon	2	7	4	2	6	3	8	5	3	7	4	4	8	Mon
Tue	3	8	5	3	7	4	9	6	4	8	5	5	9	Tue
Wed	4	9	6	4	8	5	10	7	5	9	6	6	10	Wed
Thurs	5	10	7	5	9	6	11	8	6	10	7	7	11	Thurs
Fri	6	11	8	6	10	7	12	9	7	11	8	8	12	Fri
Sat	7	12	9	7	11	8	13	10	8	12	9	9	13	Sat
Sun	8	13	10	8	12	9	14	11	9	13	10	10	14	Sun
Mon	9	14	11	9	13	10	15	12	10	14	11	11	15	Mon
Tue	10	15	12	10	14	11	16	13	11	15	12	12	16	Tue
Wed	11	16	13	11	15	12	17	14	12	16	13	13	17	Wed
Thurs	12	17	14	12	16	13	18	15	13	17	14	14	18	Thurs
Fri	13	18	15	13	17	14	19	16	14	18	15	15	19	Fri
Sat	14	19	16	14	18	15	20	17	15	19	16	16	20	Sat
Sun	15	20	17	15	19	16	21	18	16	20	17	17	21	Sun
Mon	16	21	18	16	20	17	22	19	17	21	18	18	22	Mon
Tue	17	22	19	17	21	18	23	20	18	22	19	19	23	Tue
Wed	18	23	20	18	22	19	24	21	19	23	20	20	24	Wed
Thurs	19	24	21	19	23	20	25	22	20	24	21	21	25	Thurs
Fri	20	25	22	20	24	21	26	23	21	25	22	22	26	Fri
Sat	21	26	23	21	25	22	27	24	22	26	23	23	27	Sat
Sun	22	27	24	22	26	23	28	25	23	27	24	24	28	Sun
Mon	23	28	25	23	27	24	29	26	24	28	25	25	29	Mon
Tue	24	29	26	24	28	25	30	27	25	29	26	26	30	Tue
Wed	25	30	27	25	29	26	31	28	26	30	27	27		Wed
Thurs	26	31	28	26	30	27		29	27	31	28	28		Thurs
Fri	27		29	27	31	28		30	28			20		Fri
Sat	28		30	28		29			29			30		Sat
Sun	29			29		30			30			31		Sun
Mon	30			30					31					Mon
Tue				31										Tue

Notes

Notes

Notes

Notes